MARY STUART

by FRIEDRICH SCHILLER

a new version by DAVID HARROWER

from a literal translation by Patricia Benecke

NATIONAL THEATRE OF SCOTLAND

MARY STUART Friedrich Schiller

a new version by David Harrower

CAST

Mary Stuart	Catherine Cusack
Elizabeth	Siobhan Redmond
Jane Kennedy	Eileen Walsh
Mortimer	Robin Laing
Burleigh	John Stahl
Talbot	Ralph Riach
Paulet	Ken Drury
O'Kelly / Davison	Jamie Michie
Melville / Aubespine	Roy Sampson
Kent / Bellievre / Burgoyne	Callum Cuthbertson
Leicester	Phil McKee

MARY STUART
in this new version was first performed at
CITIZENS THEATRE, GLASGOW
on Tuesday 3rd October 2006

A co-production with
the Citizens' Theatre,
Glasgow, and the
Royal Lyceum Theatre,
Edinburgh

CITIZENS THEATRE

Vicky Featherstone	Director
David Harrower	Writer
Neil Warmington	Designer / Costume Designer
Natasha Chivers	Lighting Designer
John Harris	Composer
Tom Zwitserlood	Sound Designer

TOUR DATES

CITIZENS THEATRE, GLASGOW
3rd to 21st October

ROYAL LYCEUM THEATRE, EDINBURGH
27th October to 18th November

THE PLAY

NTS Web Editor Colin Clark talks to David Harrower.

In this interview during the early stages of rehearsals for
Mary Stuart, *David Harrower discusses his personal reactions
to Schiller's classic play and describes the process of adapting
the text.*

Colin Clark *Phyllida Lloyd, who directed* Mary Stuart *last
year at the Apollo Theatre in London, said 'The play has
everything you crave from a night at the theatre: it has politics,
it has passion and it's not without a dose of irony and humour.'
Is that a good description of* Mary Stuart, *do you think?*

David Harrower I haven't seen this current production of
Mary Stuart on stage yet – and in fact, I've never actually seen
the play performed. I reacted to it when I read it – the literal
translation and also a couple of other published translations –
but to see it on stage is a totally different matter and right
now I can only hope it contains all the elements described.

I hope the audience engage with its politics, I hope they're
moved by the passion and laugh in the right places but over
the next few weeks in the rehearsal room, I'm still refining and
rewriting what began initially as my vision of the play – and
what has now become a common vision – of the director and
the actors. So the play itself is still being wrestled with and
debated over and is ever-changing. Some of the beliefs I formed
about it in the quiet of my writing room at home, about its
levels of passion, the breadth of its politics, etc., have been
tested and proved totally wrong.

I'm intrigued to find out how an audience receives the play.
It's not a tragedy in the classical sense, though it stems from
Schiller's study of the Greek dramatists, nor is it a 'history'
play – it's a strange, powerful hybrid. It does ask for quite a
deep knowledge of Elizabethan and Scottish history and this is
something we've talked about – whether not knowing some of
the references will mar engagement with it. However, we've
also attempted to make it work as a political thriller – ideology
and religious suspicion battling it out in a race against time to
save England or the head of a beloved Scots queen depending
on which side you're on.

CC Mary Stuart *was written over 200 years ago by a German –
what kind of perspective does that give us as Scots on our
history?*

DH It's an intriguing view because he's imagined a meeting between two historical queens, Mary and Elizabeth I that never actually took place. It must have been a daring leap of imagination for Schiller to attempt this and I've found myself wondering how the idea for the play came about. Was it the non-existent meeting that charged the play around it, was that the image that sparked it? Or had he been writing the play and then found himself on the edge of an abyss after Act Two: will I or won't I? He must have known he would attract voices of condemnation and criticism from Britain and Europe (not least by what was seen as his idealisation of Catholicism.)

It's conceivable that a play called *Mary Stuart* could be written with Mary and Elizabeth never meeting – that perhaps is a more modern solution – but Schiller decided to dramatically imagine it. Not, I don't think, to come to any conclusion about Mary's place or importance in Scottish history but to do with his own dramatic exploration of freedom, belief and the willingness to stand by those beliefs.

I've been asking some of my friends what they know about Mary Queen of Scots and I've been quite surprised. Although we know *of* her, I'm not sure we know exactly what she *means* to us. She holds quite a strange place in our history akin to that of Bonnie Prince Charlie. Along with him, she's a kind of icon of romantic failure, of the heart surmounting the head. And how the English treated her – locking her up for nineteen years – has never been used for any aggrieved cultural or political agenda. That part of her life, the most tragic, barring a few songs, seems to have been largely forgotten about. Not knowing what she means to us is an enduring problem – whether she should be celebrated or derided. Maybe, being Scottish, our derision of her *is* celebratory, I don't know . . .

Schiller did his best in this play to restore Mary's reputation. Or at least the reputation he thought she deserved. In many ways though, the more fascinating part is the character of Elizabeth (which ironically perhaps wasn't Schiller's intention) because she has a longer journey to complete, full of slip-sliding and moral anguish over her actions and her legitimacy and suitability for England's throne.

CC *The original text was written by Schiller and translated by Patricia Benecke – what is your role in the writing process?*

DH I was sent the literal translation – which is a close approximation of the German – and read it closely a few times. I agreed to do it because I didn't know the play before and I loved the ideas and the dramatic lifeblood of the play. I then had to ask myself, what can I do to this text? What can I bring to it? Why should I be doing this now in 2006?

Once I've answered these questions for myself, I start to do a first draft – a very general one, trying to learn the rhythms that Schiller wrote in, what he was trying to do with it. His dramatic German is dense, fluent, rhetorical – long set speeches put forth argument and counter argument. It can look very imposing on the page and my initial impulse was to take a machete to it, to hack through what very quickly became irritating. But it's always the way, you begin to hate the literal translation because you know it's your guide but you're also wanting to break free from it, to walk unaided, to stamp your creative authority onto it. So invariably I arrived at a kind of 'limbo' draft, that had precious little of Schiller in it, and precious little of myself.

I then let Vicky look at the first draft and we talked about it at length and I went away again and completed a second draft which is usually where it all begins to come together. A voice, a tone have been found – aspects that you would think would come easily but rarely do when you're adapting another writer's text. Practically every word has to be held up, examined, tested – is it too modern? Too archaic? Will it disrupt the play? The rhythm you've found? What does a sentence say about its speaker? What do the words he or she use reveal about them?

When people ask me what it is I actually do, what 'a new version by' actually means, the best I can do is say that I write . . . not literally, but figuratively, on tracing paper, glimpsing the play below me as I work, always aware of its presence. My aim is to transmute the language – refracted through the English translation from Schiller's German, to render it anew and capture the play's essence. This means finding a suitable style and tone – one that a modern ear could accommodate which still held a poetic sensibility to it – while releasing the forward propulsion of the drama.

Lastly, I have to say, that no matter how gleaming or polished I make my adapted text, the most crucial work gets done in the rehearsal room with the director and all the actors standing over it, keeping close, guarding watch over their characters' progress through the play. This is when Schiller's stagecraft gets tested, when the dialogue I've decided on is communally improved or cut, when the architecture of this great play is properly revealed to all of us.

THE COMPANY

DAVID HARROWER (Writer)

David Harrower lives in Glasgow. His first play *Knives in Hens* was premiered at the Traverse Theatre in 1995, the production transferring to the Bush Theatre later that year. In 1997 it was produced in Berlin by Thomas Ostermeier at the Deutsch Theatre, Berlin, where it ran for three years, winning the 1998 Theater Heute Best Foreign Play. Since then it has been staged in twenty countries worldwide.

Other plays include *Kill the Old, Torture Their Young* (Traverse, 1998) which won the 1999 Meyer-Whitworth Award and the Pearson Award; *The Chrysalids* (NT Connections); *Presence* (Royal Court, 2001), *Dark Earth* (Traverse, 2003) and most recently, *Blackbird* (Edinburgh International Festival, 2005), directed by Peter Stein. The production subsequently transferred to London's West End. *Blackbird* was shortlisted for the Saltire Society Book of the Year Award 2005.

Adaptations include: Pirandello's *Six Characters in Search of an Author* (Young Vic, 2001), Büchner's *Woyzeck* (Royal Lyceum, 2001), Chekhov's *Ivanov* (National Theatre, 2002) and *Tales From the Vienna Woods* by Horvath (National Theatre, 2003).

NATASHA CHIVERS (Lighting Designer)

Theatre work includes: *The Wolves In The Walls, HOME Glasgow* (National Theatre of Scotland), *Sunday in the Park with George* (Wyndham's Theatre/Chocolate Factory), *A Fine Balance* (Tamasha/Hampstead Theatre), *Jerusalem, Playhouse Creatures, My Mother Said I Never Should,* (West Yorkshire Playhouse), *Renaissance* (Greenwich and Docklands International Festival), *Dirty Wonderland,* (Frantic Assembly/Brighton Festival), *Who's Afraid of Virginia Wolf* (Liverpool Playhouse), *Hymns* (Frantic Assembly/Lyric Hammersmith/tour), *The Paines Plough Season* at The Chocolate Factory including *Mercury Fur* (with Plymouth Drum), *Pyrenees* (Paines Plough/Tron), *If Destroyed Still True* (Dundee Rep) and *Small Things, The Unexpected Man, Present Laughter* (Bath Theatre Royal/tour), *The Bomb-itty of Errors* (The New Ambassadors), *The Straits* (Paines Plough/Hampstead Theatre/59 East 59, New York), *Beauty Queen of Leenane* (Watford Palace), *Liverpool Everyman 40th Anniversary Season* including *Urban Legend* and *The Kindness of Strangers, Ma Rainey's Black Bottom* and *The Entertainer* (Liverpool Playhouse), *Who's Afraid of the Big Bad Book* (Soho Theatre/Warwick Arts Centre), *The Cherry Orchard* and *After The Dance* (Oxford Stage Company/tour), *Peepshow* (Frantic Assembly, Plymouth Theatre Royal, Lyric Hammersmith and tour), *The Drowned World* (Paines Plough, Traverse and Bush Theatre), *Tiny Dynamite* (Frantic Assembly/Paines Plough).

CATHERINE CUSACK
(Mary Stuart)

Theatre work includes: *The Factory Girls* (Arcola Theatre), *The Mushroom Pickers* (Southwark Playhouse), *Bronte* (Shared Experience), *The Gigli Concert* (Finborough Theatre), *The Gentleman from Olmedo* and *The Venetian Twins* (Newbury Watermill Theatre), *The Increased Difficulty of Concentration* (Gate Theatre), *Blood Red, Saffron Yellow* (Plymouth Theatre Royal), *Our Lady Of Sligo*, (Out of Joint/National Theatre), *Measure For Measure* (English Touring Theatre), *Prayers Of Sherkin* (Peter Hall Company), *Mrs Warren's Profession* (Lyric Hammersmith), *Phaedra's Love* (Gate Theatre), *Mill on the Floss* (Shared Experience), *The Glass Menagerie* (Bolton Octagon Theatre), *Brighton Rock* (West Yorkshire Playhouse), *Moonlight, You Never Can Tell, The Seagull* (Gate Theatre), *Bold Girls* (Hampstead Theatre), *Lovers' Meetings* (Druid), *Poor Beast in the Rain* (Bush Theatre), *Les Liaisons Dangereuses* (Ambassadors), *Germinal* (Paines Plough), *The Hostage* (Tricycle Theatre).

Television work includes: *Jonathan Creek, Dr Who* (BBC), *Ballykissangel*, (BBC TV/World Productions), *Coronation Street* (Granada Television), *Cadfael, The Bill, The Chief, Sofia and Constance.*

Film work includes: *Conspiracy Of Silence* (Firefly Films), *Finding Neverland* (Film Colony), *The Lonely Passion of Judith Hearne* (Handmade Films).

CALLUM CUTHBERTSON
(Kent/Bellievre/Burgoyne)

Theatre work includes: *Home Dumfries* (National Theatre of Scotland), *Rain, Cinders, Quartet* (*Oran Mor*), *The Graduate, Dumbstruck, Scenes From An Execution* (Dundee Rep), *Habitats* (Tron/EK Performance), *Cinderella* (Tron), *Lamcent* (Suspect Culture/Toronto Six Stages), *San Diego* (Tron/Edinburgh International Festival), *Love Freaks* (Tron), *The Good Person of Sechzuan* (Tag).

Television work includes: *Legit* (Comedy Unit/ BBC Scotland), *Jess the Border Collie, Intergalactic Kitchen* (BBC Scotland), *Rockface* (BBC).

Film work includes: *The End of the Sentence* (Tartan Short), *Grockle Dance* (Violet Films), *How High the Castle Wall,* (Fallingwater Films).

KEN DRURY (Paulet)

Theatre work includes: *Henry IV* (RSC), *View From the Bridge* and *Titus Andronicus* (Bristol Old Vic), *King Lear, Rosmersholm, The Mysteries, Macbeth, The Crucible* (National Theatre), *All My Sons* (Wyndhams Theatre), *Mutiny!* (Piccadilly Theatre), *As You Like It* (Ludlow Festival), *The Price* (Royal Lyceum), *The Three Musketeers* (Sheffield Crucible Theatre), *The Power of Darkness* (The Orange Tree), *The Colour Of Justice* (Tricycle Theatre), *Disposing of the Body* (Hampstead Theatre), *Cinderella* (King's Theatre), *The Father's Suit, The Prisoner* (Oran Mor).

Television work includes: *A Sense of Freedom, Dr. Findlay, Taggart* (STV), *Rab C Nesbit, Strathblair, Dangerfield, Only Fools and Horses, Down Among the Big Boys, Brokers Men, Hamish Macbeth, Holby City, Monarch of the Glen, The Bell Rock, Sea of Souls* (BBC), *September Song, Bloodlines, The Eleventh Hour* (Granada), *Inspector Morse, Kavanagh QC, London's Burning, Under the Sun, Heartbeat, A Is for Acid, A Touch of Frost* (ITV), *Relic Hunters* (Fireworks Entertainment), *The Last Detective* (Meridian Television), *Foyle's War* (Greenlit Films), *Psychos, Life on Mars* (Kudos Films), *The Boyhood of John Muir* (US TV Florentine Films) *Shackleton* (First Sight Productions).

Film work includes: *Yanks, The Ploughman's Lunch, Venus Peter, The Big Man.* Also *Four Weddings and a Funeral* (Working Title Films) *Janice Beard* (Dakota Films), *Women Talking Dirty* (Rocket Productions), *Simon Magus* (Silesia Films), *Shadows in the Sun* (Studio 8 Productions), *Lassie* (First Sight Films).

VICKY FEATHERSTONE (Director)

Vicky joined the National Theatre of Scotland in November 2004 from Paines Plough Theatre Company in London. Her work at Paines Plough included: *Pyrenees, The Small Things, The Drowned World, Crazy Gary's Mobile Disco, Tiny Dynamite, Splendour* and *Crave.*

The recipient of 12 theatre awards in the past six years alone, Vicky is also well known for bringing a number of critically acclaimed productions to the Edinburgh Festival Fringe over many years and her work with Graeae Theatre Company, which presents productions by people with physical and sensory impairments.

JOHN HARRIS (Composer)

John Harris is the director of internet-based music company Seven Things and performs and writes with his multi-instrumental group SPKE.

Theatre work includes: *Julie* (National Theatre of Scotland), *Jerusalem* (West Yorkshire Playhouse), *East Coast Chicken Supper, The Nest, Family, Kill the Old Torture their Young, Perfect Days, Greta, Knives in Hens, Anna Weiss, Sharp Shorts* (Traverse), *Solstice, Midwinter* (RSC), *Il Bellissimo Silencio, Of Nettles and Roses, Stockaree* (Theatre Workshop), *Drummers* (Out of Joint).

Film and TV work include: *Paternoster, The Emperor* (C4), *The Green Man of Knowledge* (S4C).

ROBIN LAING (Mortimer)

Robin trained at Dundee College and Fife College.

Theatre work includes: *Slope* (Untitled/Tramway), *Elizabeth Gordon Quinn* (National Theatre of Scotland), *As You Like It* (Royal Lyceum), *Invention of Love* (Salisbury

Playhouse), *Medea* (US Tour, Broadway and Paris), *A Midsummer Night's Dream, Loot* (Manchester Royal Exchange), *Skylight* (Perth Theatre), *The Mill Lavies* (Dundee Rep), *Trainspotting* (UK and West End tour).

Television work includes: *Murder City* (Granada TV), *Born and Bred, Waking the Dead, Into the Blue, Murder Rooms, The Lakes, The Lakes II* (BBC), *Band of Brothers* (HBO/Dreamworks), *Relative Strangers* (Little Bird), *Heaven on Earth, Deadly Summer* (Red Rooster Productions), *Taggart* (STV), *Cadfael III* (Carlton TV).

Film work includes: *Joyeaux Noel* (Nord-Ouest Films), *Joy Rider* (Classic Film Productions), *Borstal Boys* (Hell's Kitchen), *The Slab Boys* (Skreba/Slab Boys).

PHIL MCKEE (Leicester)

Phil trained at RSAMD.

Theatre work includes: *Strawberries in January* (Traverse), *A Madman Sings to the Moon, Julius Caesar* (Royal Lyceum), *Damages* (Bush Theatre), *8000M* (Suspect Culture), *Stitching* (Red Room/The Bush Theatre), *Macbeth* (The Cage Theatre Company), *The Robbers, The Boat Plays* (The Gate), *Richard III, Napoli Milionaria, King Lear* (National Theatre) and *Lady Betty* (Cheek By Jowl).

Television work includes: *Ghost Squad* (Company Pictures/Channel 4), *The Family, The Place of the Dead* (LWT), *Band of Brothers* (HBO/BBC), *Lost in France, Silent Witness, Lovejoy* (BBC), *The Bill* (Thames), *Heartbeat* (YTV), *Crime Traveller* (Carnival/BBC), *Richard II* (Illuminations), *Soldier Soldier* (Carlton TV) and *Taggart* (STV).

Film work includes: *George & the Dragon* (Carousel), *The Lost Battalion* (Carousel/A&E), *Joan of Arc* (Leeloo Productions), *Beginners Luck, Simon Magus* (Silesia Films/Channel 4), *The Debt Collector* (Dragon Pictures) and *The Star* (Renegage Films).

JAMIE MICHIE (O'Kelly/Davidson)

Jamie trained at LAMDA.

Theatre work includes: *The Real Thing* (Northampton Theatre Royal), *Romeo and Juliet* (Cork Opera House), *The Houghmagandie Pack* (Grid Iron), *Howie The Rookie* (Forth Road).

Television work includes: *Feel The Force* (Catherine Baily Productions), *Ultimate Force* (Bentley Productions), *Holby City, Alexei Sayle, Let's Dance, Redcaps* (BBC), *Footballers' Wives* (Shed Productions), *Rock Face* (BBC Scotland), *Swallow* (Box TV for Channel 4).

Film work includes: *Trout* (Tartan Shorts).

SIOBHAN REDMOND (Elizabeth)

Siobhan trained at Bristol Old Vic Theatre School.

Theatre work includes: *Les Liaisons Dangereuses, Us and*

Them (Hampstead Theatre), *The Prime Of Miss Jean Brodie* (Royal Lyceum), *Perfect Days* (West End/Hampstead/Traverse), *Spanish Tragedy, Much Ado About Nothing* (RSC), *An Experienced Woman Gives Advice* (Manchester Royal Exchange), *The Trick is to Keep Breathing* (Tron/Royal Court/Toronto), *King Lear, A Midsummer Night's Dream* (Renaissance Theatre Company), *The Lunatic Queen* (Riverside Studio).

Television work includes: *The Smoking Room, Sea of Souls, Holby City, In the Red, Nervous Energy, Between the Lines, Wokenwell* (LWT), *Throwaways, Deacon Brodie, The High Life* (BBC).

RALPH RIACH (Talbot)

Theatre work includes: *Jack and the Beanstalk* (Eden Court), *Run For Your Wife* (Scottish tour), *Don't Tell The Wife* (King's, Edinburgh), *Lock Up Your Daughters* (Perth Theatre), *Breeksadoon* (Also Toured Germany), *Dead Men* (Traverse), *McQuin's Metamorphosis, Losing Venice* (Traverse/Australia and Hong Kong), *Elizabeth Gordon Quinn, Pygmalion, A Midsummer Night's Dream* (Royal Lyceum), *The Grand Edinburgh Fire Balloon, Cinderella* (Pavilion), *Dead Dad Dog* (Traverse), *The Way We Were, City Lights* (tour), *Elizabeth Gordon Quinn, Judy* (Perth Theatre), *Peter Pan* (Eden Court), *A Voyage Round Parahandy* (Byre), *What Every Woman Knows* (Perth Theatre), *Death of a Salesman/The Last Yankee* (West Yorkshire Playhouse), *Dumbstruck* (Tron), *A Christmas Carol* (Communicado/Tron), *A Christmas Carol* (Byre).

TV work includes: *Lost Empires* (Granada TV), *First Among Equals, Watching, Taggart* (STV), *Take The High Road, Dr Finlay, Tutti Frutti* (BBC), *Byrne On Byrne, Changing Step, Clarissa, Rides, Casualty, Spender, City Lights, Deacon Brodie, Chancer* (Central), *The Bill* (Thames), *Ball on the Slates* (C4), *Hamish Macbeth* (BBC), *Peak Practice* (Carlton), *Randall And Hopkirk Deceased* (Ghost Prods), *Brotherly Love* (BBC Scotland), *Monarch of the Glen* (Ecosse), *A Tinker's Holiday* (Ronan O'Leary Prods), *Murder Rooms* (BBC), *The Russian Bride* (ITV), *Brotherly Love II* (BBC Scotland), *Tinsel Town II* (Raindog Television for BBC), *Taggart* (SMG), *The Canterbury Tales – The Miller's Tale* (BBC), *The Night Detective* (Zenith North Productions), *Quite Ugly One Morning* (Quite Ugly Films), *Inter-galactic Patrick* (Tiger Lily Productions for BBC), *The House That God Built* (BBC), *The Strange Case of Sherlock Holmes, Scottish Enlighten-ment, Ruby In The Smoke* (BBC), *Low Winter Sun* (Tiger Aspect/C4).

Film work includes: *The Big Man, Latin For A Dark Room* (Goldstar Prods), *Braveheart* (Warner Brothers), *The Honest Courtesan* (Bedford Falls), *In Praise of Older Women* (Lola Films), *Doom And Gloom, My Life So Far* (Enigma Prods), *The Governess* (Parallax Films), *Nurse Ajax*

(Compulsive Viewing), *Darkness in the Afternoon* (Cormorant Prods), *Joan Of Arc* (Leeloo Prods), *The House of Mirth* (Three Rivers), *Anazapta* (Anazapta Films/Entreprise Films), *The Rocket Post* (Ultimate Pictures), *The Bum's Rush* (Scot Three Ltd), *Blinded* (Blinded Ltd.), *Copying Beethoven* (Sidney Kimmel Entertainment).

Radio work includes various plays and stories for BBC Radio Scotland and Radio 4.

ROY SAMPSON
(Melvil/Aubespin)

Roy trained at RSAMD.

Theatre work includes: *What Every Woman Knows* (Manchester Royal Exchange), *Amazonia* (Bridewell Theatre), *Canterbury Tales* (Duke's Playhouse), *See You Next Tuesday* (Albery Theatre), *The Suppliants* (Gate Theatre), The Three Musketeers (New Vic Theatre).

Television work includes: *New Tricks, The Message, Sea of Souls, Holding On, St Antony's Day Off, The Last Duel* (BBC), *God's Messengers* (Granada Television), *Dr Finlay, Taggart* (STV).

Film work includes: *Infinite Justice, If Only, Perfect, House of Mirth, Hellbound.*

JOHN STAHL
(Lord Burleigh)

John trained at RSAMD.

Theatre work includes: *The Crucible* (RSC/West End) *Alice Trilogy* (Royal Court), *Blue Eyes and Heels* (Soho Theatre), *Professor Bernhardi* (Dumbfounded Theatre), *The Found Man* (Traverse), *Dog In the Manger, Tamar's Revenge, Pedro* (RSC), *Bread And Butter, Sergeant Musgrave's Dance* (Oxford Stage Company), *Mr Placebo* (Traverse/Theatre Royal Plymouth), *Crave* (Paines Plough), *Gagarin Way* (Arts Theatre West End), *The Magic Toyshop* (Shared Experience), *The Weir* (Royal Court), *The Meeting, Anna Weiss* (Traverse), *All My Sons* (Theatre Royal Plymouth), *The Jock Stein Story* (Glasgow Pavilion), *Hamlet* (Belgrade Theatre, Coventry).

Television work includes: *Doctors, Darien Venture, Murder Rooms* (BBC), *Glasgow Kiss* (Channel 4), *High Road, Doctor Finlay* (STV), *Resort to Murder* (London Films).

Film work includes: *Loch Ness* (Working Title).

EILEEN WALSH
(Jane Kennedy)

Theatre work includes: *The Merchant Of Venice, Phaedra's Love* (Corcadorca), *Portia Coughlan, Ariel* (Abbey Theatre), *Crave* (Royal Court Theatre), *The Drowned World* (Traverse), *Splendour* (Paines Plough) *Troilus And Cressida* (Oxford Stage Company), *Boomtown* (Rough Magic/Dublin Theatre Festival), *Disco Pigs* (Bush Theatre/Arts Theatre), *Danti Dan* (Rough Magic/Hampstead Theatre), *Crestfall* (Dublin Gate Theatre), *The Entertainer* (Liverpool Playhouse).

Television work includes: *Pure Mule* (Eden Films).

Film work includes: *Nicholas Nickleby* (United Artists), *Magdalene Sisters* (Momentum), *When Brendan Met Trudy* (Deadly Films), *Miss Julie* (Red Mullet Productions), *Janice Beard* (Dakota Films), *The Last Bus Home* (Bandit Films), *Spaghetti Slow* (McFilms), *The Van* (Deadly Films).

NEIL WARMINGTON
(Set & Costume Designer)

Neil graduated in fine art painting from Maidstone College of Art before attending the Motley Theatre Design course in London.

Work includes: *The Straits* (Hampstead/New York), *The Drowned World, Splendour, Riddance, Crazy Horse, The Small Things, Pyrenees, If Destroyed True* (Paines Plough), *Playhouse Creatures* (West Yorkshire Playhouse), *King Lear* (English Touring Theatre/Old Vic), *Ghosts, Don Juan, John Gabriel Borkman, Taming of the Shrew, Love's Labour Lost* (English Touring Theatre), *Scenes from an Execution, Dumbstruck, Lie of the Mind, Gypsy, The Talented Mr Ripley* (Dundee Rep), *Woyzeck, The Glass Menagerie, Comedians, Tankred Dorst's Merlin* (Royal Lyceum), *Solemn Mass for a Full Moon in Summer, Family, Passing Places, King of the Fields, Gagarin Way, Slab Boys Trilogy,* (Traverse), *Knives in Hens, The Birthday Party, A Taste of Honey,* (TAG and national tour), *Angels in America* (7:84), *Life's A Dream, Fiddler on the Roof* (West Yorkshire Playhouse), *Henry V* (RSC), *Much Ado About Nothing* (Queen's London), *Sunset Song, Mary Queen of Scots Got Her head Chopped Off* (Theatre Royal), *The Life of Stuff* (Donmar), *Waiting for Godot, Much Ado About Nothing* (Liverpool Everyman), *The Tempest* (Contact), *Jane Eyre, Desire Under the Elms* (Shared Experience), *Troilus and Cressida* (Opera North), *Oedipus Rex – Stravinsky* (Connecticut State Opera), *The Marriage of Figaro* (Garsington Opera).

TOM ZWITSERLOOD
(Sound Designer)

Tom Zwitserlood was born in The Netherlands. He has been Head of Sound at the Royal Lyceum Theatre in Edinburgh since 2001, and is responsible for most of their and the Lyceum Youth Theatre's sound designs. Tom has also worked on a great variety of other theatre productions as sound designer or engineer. Credits include *The Woman Who Cooked Her Husband, Two* and *Realism* (National Theatre of Scotland). Before moving to Scotland Tom worked in The Netherlands as a sound technician for one of their renowned drama companies Het Zuidelijk Toneel.

[NATIONAL THEATRE OF SCOTLAND]

Scottish theatre has always been for the people, led by great performances, great stories or great playwrights. The National Theatre of Scotland exists to build a new generation of theatre-goers as well as reinvigorating the existing ones; to create theatre on a national and international scale that is contemporary, confident and forward-looking; to bring together brilliant artists, composers, choreographers and playwrights; and to exceed expectations of what and where theatre can be.

The National Theatre of Scotland has no building. Instead, we are taking theatre all over Scotland, working with the existing venues, touring and creating work within the theatre community. We have no bricks-and mortar institutionalism to counter, nor the security of a permanent home in which to develop. All our money and energy can be spent on creating the work. Our theatre will take place in the great buildings – Edinburgh's Royal Lyceum and Glasgow's Citizens' Theatre – but also in site specific locations, community halls and drill halls, car parks and forests.

Since our launch in February 2006 we have produced:

- *HOME* – an extraordinary opening event which took place in ten locations across the country

- *FALLING* – a promenading site-specific performance co-produced with Poorboy

- *THE WOLVES IN THE WALLS* – a musical pandemonium for all the family co-produced with Improbable

- *ROAM* – a site-specific event at Edinburgh Airport co-produced with Grid Iron

- *THE CRUCIBLE* – a touring professional and community cast event co-produced with TAG

- *ELIZABETH GORDON QUINN* – a major revival of Chris Hannan's Scottish classic

- *BLACK WATCH* – an unauthorized biography of the legendary Scottish regiment

- *REALISM* – a world premiere of Anthony Neilson's new work co-produced with the Edinburgh International Festival

- *ENSEMBLE* – a company of seven performers touring towns and villages across the country with a repertory of three plays: *JULIE* adapted by Zinnie Harris from the Strindberg play; *MANCUB* by Douglas Maxwell; and *GOBBO* devised and created by David Greig and Wils Wilson.

During these inaugural six months we have won a clutch of awards. At the Critics' Awards for Theatre in Scotland, we won Best Ensemble, Best Technical Presentation and Best Theatre Production for *ROAM,* Best Children's Show and Best Design for *HOME: East Lothian* and Best Music for *HOME: Shetland.* In August we became the first company to appear at both the Edinburgh International and Fringe Festivals, receiving a Herald Angel for *REALISM* and a Herald Angel, a Fringe First, a List Best Theatre Writing Award and a Stage Award for Best Ensemble for *BLACK WATCH.*

This autumn, along with *MARY STUART,* we are also touring a new stage version of John Byrne's *TUTTI FRUTTI,* and *PROJECT MACBETH,* an NTS Learn production.

For more information about
the National Theatre of Scotland, visit
www.nationaltheatrescotland.com
or call +44 (0) 141 221 0970

Scottish
Arts Council

CITIZENS THEATRE

The Citizens' Theatre was founded in 1943 by James Bridie and has been Scotland's flagship theatre for more than sixty years. The company has a distinguished history, presenting an extraordinary world repertoire and nurturing the talent of many of Scotland's finest artists. Today it produces an unrivalled range of work, presenting more home grown productions annually than any other theatre in Scotland.

The Citizens' Theatre is based in the heart of the Gorbals. The location of the Citizens' is both unique and crucial to its identity. The Theatre works extensively with the local community, and in recent years has nurtured a Community Company, a Cultural Diversity Company (latterly merged into the Community Company) and a Young Co. The Theatre is essential to the cultural and economic revival of a diverse area of Glasgow which still faces significant social and economic challenges.

The Citizens' Theatre's reputation contributed significantly to the City of Glasgow's successful bid to be City of Culture in 1990, the lasting cultural and economic effect of which is still being felt today.

The Citizens' Theatre Company is now entering an ambitious new era of expansion. From April 2007 the Citizens' Theatre will work together with TAG, its sister company. TAG has led the way in Scotland in its work for young people and children for more than 30 years. The Company offers an exceptionally broad range of highest quality productions and participatory projects designed to engage and inspire Scotland's children and young people. Founded in 1967, TAG is the longest-established touring theatre company in Scotland. As such, the company draws upon unparalleled experience in generating memorable creative experiences for young citizens both within and outwith the formal education sector.

Thinking and planning together under the joint Artistic Directorship of Jeremy Raison and Guy Hollands, the new Company will further develop the Citizens' Theatre's hugely successful work on stage, in schools and in communities. Creative learning and participation will be at its heart. The integration of TAG and the Citizens' Theatre will create a new model, enabling the Company to offer its audiences a fully-rounded theatre experience, from participation and creative learning experiences through to attendance at theatre productions that can travel the world.

Jeremy Raison and Guy Hollands, Artistic Directors

THE LYCEUM
Royal Lyceum Theatre Edinburgh

The Royal Lyceum Theatre Company (the Lyceum) is one of Scotland's leading producing drama companies, with a strong reputation for excellence in both classical and contemporary work. It is committed to developing the country's considerable indigenous talents while presenting the best of international drama to the public. The Lyceum aims to reach a wide audience, whatever their age or experience of theatre going, and to enable them to access the richly imaginative world of drama. With a seating capacity of 658, the theatre building is a magnificent example of late Victorian architecture. The Lyceum is a unique venue for events and functions.

We present between 7-10 productions a year and collaborate in major festivals including the Edinburgh International and Children's Festivals. Audience figures are impressive: 3,000 season subscribers come to every show; and over 130,000 people attend our theatre each year.

The Lyceum's policy is to develop a local, UK and international profile. This includes commissioning new work, staging contemporary plays and producing classics of world theatre. The Lyceum has recently staged co-productions with Theatre Royal, Bath, The Bush Theatre, London, Nottingham Playhouse Theatre Company and Belgrade Theatre, Coventry. The 2005 production of Laurel & Hardy was invited to the Dublin Theatre Festival in September that year. The Lyceum is delighted to be working with the National Theatre of Scotland and the Citizens Theatre, Glasgow.

Our educational work is both in-house and outreach. Resource Packs are produced linked to productions and these go to the growing number of schools who benefit from our activities. The Lyceum Youth Theatre is widely regarded as one of the best youth theatres in the country.

Since Mark Thomson took over as Artistic Director in 2003 the Royal Lyceum Theatre Company has produced several award-winning productions:

CATS Award for Best Ensemble – *Six Black Candles* (2004)

CATS Award for Best Technical Presentation for *Anna Karenina* (2005),

CATS Award for Best Actor – David Tennant for Jimmy Porter in *Look Back in Anger* (2005)

Friedrich Schiller
Mary Stuart

a new version by
DAVID HARROWER
from a literal translation by Patricia Benecke

faber and faber

First published in 2006
by Faber and Faber Limited
3 Queen Square, London WC1N 3AU

Typeset by Country Setting, Kingsdown, Kent CT14 8ES
Printed in England by Bookmarque, Croydon, Surrey

A CIP record for this book
is available from the British Library

ISBN 978–0–571–23618–3
ISBN 0–571–23618–9

2 4 6 8 10 9 7 5 3 1

Characters

Mary Stuart, Queen of Scotland

Elizabeth, Queen of England

Leicester

Burleigh, Lord High Treasurer

Shrewsbury

Kent

Paulet, Mary's guardian

Mortimer, his nephew

Davison, Secretary of State

Jane Kennedy, Mary's maid

Aubespine, French Ambassador

Bellievre, French Envoy

Melville, Mary's former house steward

O'Kelly, Mortimer's accomplice

Burgoyne, Mary's doctor

Guard

Page

Act One

A room in Fotheringay Castle. Jane Kennedy, the maid of Mary, Queen of Scots, confronts Amyas Paulet as he's about to break open a cupboard.

Kennedy What're you doing? Don't touch that! This is outrageous . . .

Paulet Where did this jewellery come from? It was thrown from an upper window – to bribe the gardener, no doubt. The cunning of you women . . . I have you watched, I have you searched, but you still have valuables hidden away. There'll be more wherever this came from.

He pulls the cupboard open, takes out several papers.

Kennedy Those are her private papers!

Paulet I know.

Kennedy Nothing important – only jottings to pass the time in this prison.

Paulet That's the time when evil minds thrive.

Kennedy They're written in French.

Paulet French is the language of England's enemies . . .

He rifles through the papers.

Kennedy Those are drafts of letters to the Queen of England.

Paulet Then I shall hand them on. What's this?

He's found a secret drawer; opens it, takes out more jewellery.

A royal coronet, set with French lilies . . . It can go with the rest.

Kennedy The injustice we suffer . . .

Paulet Her hands have to be kept empty – everything she touches turns into a weapon against us.

Kennedy Who'd think the Queen of Scots is kept inside these bare walls? Where's the Canopy of State over her throne? And My Lady's soft, elegant feet must walk this rough, common floor to a table laid with pewter so coarse even the meanest noblewoman would refuse it.

Paulet It was good enough for her husband, Darnley, to drink from while she and her lover drank from gold.

Kennedy There's not even a mirror in our cell.

Paulet Every look at herself would feed her hope and daring.

Kennedy Or books to divert the mind.

Paulet She has the Bible – to better herself.

Kennedy And her lute taken from her.

Paulet She played provocative songs on it.

Kennedy This is no life for a gentle-born woman who was crowned a Queen in her cradle, and raised in the glittering, elegant court of Catherine de Medici. It's not enough you rob her of her power, you also stoop to confiscate her possessions. She'll learn to live with her misfortune, but to be allowed no comforts . . .

Paulet She should spend the time reflecting – and repenting. Denial and humiliation can help atone for a vice-ridden life.

Kennedy If she made mistakes in her youth, that's between her and God. She should not be judged here – England has no right.

Paulet England is where she committed treason, England is where she'll be judged.

Kennedy How could she when she's so closely guarded?

Paulet She was still able to reach her arm out into the nation and light the flames of civil war, arming assassins against our Queen, God save her. She induced him, that murderous coward, Babington, inspired him with letters from behind these walls. And Norfolk – iron bars weren't enough to stop her seducing Norfolk. One of this country's wisest men sacrificed to the executioner's axe. And does it stop the madmen? No. They still rush headlong towards death for her cause. The scaffolds are never empty – the blood never stops running. It'll only end with her, when she herself is executed – the guiltiest of them all. It was a cursed day when our country showed its hospitality to your Helen of Troy.

Kennedy *Hospitality?* My poor Lady was an exile – she came seeking protection from her royal cousin. Your country's 'hospitality' has been incarceration since the first day she arrived, breaking every law of nations and royal accord. And then to summon her before a court like some common criminal.

Paulet She was already a murderer when she arrived here. Her own people drove her from the throne – a throne she disgraced. She came here – jealous of England's contentment – to drag us back to the dark, bloody days of Spanish Mary, to turn England Catholic and sell us to the French.

Why did she refuse to sign the Edinburgh treaty? Why not give up her claim to England's throne? One stroke of a pen and the gates would open. But no, she prefers this prison, seeing herself wronged, clinging on to her empty title, believing she'll conquer this island from her cell.

7

Kennedy You think that's what she does here – dreams up these plans? She's buried alive behind bricks! Denied any word of comfort or voices of friendship from her home country. She sees no human face except your surly features, and that boorish young nephew of yours you've brought to help guard her. Are iron bars not enough?

Paulet How do I know she's not filing through them? The floor, these walls, they could be hollow inside – letting in treachery as I sleep. I curse this post – keeping watch over a woman like her. I wake every night fearful and walk up and down the corridors like a tortured ghost, first checking all the locks, then checking the loyalty of the jailers, dreading every day that dawns will prove me right. I hope it will be over soon. I'd rather stand guard at the gates of Hell than over your scheming monarch.

Kennedy She's coming now.

Paulet Carrying Christ in her hand as pride and lust burn in her heart . . .

SCENE TWO

Mary enters, veiled, a crucifix in her hand. Kennedy rushes to her.

Kennedy We can't be treated like this. They just walk over us. Humiliate us more every day.

Mary Calm yourself.

Kennedy He broke into your cupboard. He took letters and your bridal jewellery.

Mary They're trinkets, Jane – a Queen can live without them. I've learnt to endure a great deal in England, I can endure this. You've taken by force, Sir, what I intended to hand over to you. One of those is a letter written to my royal sister. Will you give me your word you will deliver it to her and not into Burleigh's grasping hands?

Paulet I will decide what's done with it.

Mary To save you the trouble, it asks a favour – to meet and talk with her. The cousin I've still to see with my own eyes.

I was tried in front of forty-two of her commissioners but I refuse to recognise them. Elizabeth and I are of the same family – she's of my sex and my standing. I will only speak to her.

Paulet My Lady, you are adept at placing your fate and honour in the hands of men less than worthy of your respect.

Mary I have a second favour – to refuse it would be inhumane. I am denied the consolation of my Church's holy sacraments. She's stolen my crown and my freedom, now she threatens my life. Does she also want the gates of Heaven closed to my soul?

Paulet At your request, the local dean . . .

Mary I want no dean! I demand a priest from my own Church. I demand also a secretary and notaries. The misery of this prison gnaws at my life. My days are numbered – I am a woman dying.

Paulet That is something you should contemplate.

Mary But who knows, some quick English hand may be planning to bring death sooner. I want to draw up my last will – divide out what is still mine.

Paulet You will be allowed to. The Queen of England will not want to take what belongs to you.

9

Mary Where are my chambermaids, my servants – what's happened to them? I don't need their service – only to know if they're suffering, if they lack anything.

Paulet They're provided for.

He starts to leave.

Mary You leave me again, Sir, with the agony of uncertainty. I'm cut off from the world – your spies do their job well. No news of what's to happen to me reaches through these walls. It's been a month – a long, painful month – since the commissioners descended upon me here, set up their benches and made me stand unprepared before their illegal court, to respond to slyly worded charges. They came and went like phantoms – and only silence since. I can't read your eyes. Have I been judged innocent or not? Tell me! Let me know what I should fear or what I should hope.

Paulet I'd suggest you make your peace with Heaven.

Mary I pray for Heaven's mercy, Sir – but it may be too much to expect justice from my earthly judges . . .

Paulet You shall have justice, don't doubt that.

Mary Is my case decided?

Paulet I don't know.

Mary Am I condemned to die?

Paulet I know nothing, My Lady.

Mary You like things done quickly here – maybe a murderer will descend on me just like the commissioners did. Nothing would surprise me now, no judgement made by a Westminster tribunal driven by Burleigh's hate and Hatton's zeal. I know very well what England's Queen has the power to command.

Paulet England's monarchs listen only to their conscience and their Parliament. When judgement has been passed, the world shall see the sentence carried out.

SCENE THREE

Mortimer enters. Ignoring Mary, he addresses Paulet.

Mortimer Uncle. They're here.

He exits. Paulet makes to leave.

Mary Sir, I listen to what you say, I respect your age – but this boy . . . I cannot bear his ignorance and impertinence.

Paulet What you find odious in him, I admire. He's no weak-hearted fool, easily softened by female tears. He's a travelled man – recently to Paris and Rheims – and in him beats a staunch English heart. Your artful approaches will be wasted on him, My Lady.

He exits.

SCENE FOUR

Mary, Kennedy.

Kennedy How he can speak to your face like that? It's too much.

Mary (*lost in thought*) In days past I listened too willingly to flattery. Perhaps I deserve it, to hear only hostile voices now.

Kennedy My Lady, don't lose heart . . . You're the cheerful one – you always had to comfort me, remember?

Mary I can see him, Jane. It's Darnley's ghost – it's risen from the grave to taunt me. This will never end until he's destroyed me.

Kennedy Don't think these thoughts.

Mary I've too good a memory. Today's the anniversary of his death. That's why my penitence and fasting – in commemoration.

Kennedy You have to lay this to rest. You've repented for too many years – made yourself suffer. The Church has forgiven you. Heaven has forgiven you.

Mary The guilt will never be buried – it will always bleed out of me. Darnley wants revenge. A server's bell won't send him back, or a priest holding a cross.

Kennedy You didn't murder him.

Mary I knew about it. I let it happen. I lured him to his death with my promise of love.

Kennedy You were so young – too young to take on such guilt.

Mary It weighs so heavily on me – it always has.

Kennedy It was his fault – *his* insults, *his* arrogance. You raised him from obscurity, blessed him with your radiance, led him from your bed to your throne and your crown. You *created* him – and how did he thank you? Mistreated you, disrespected you – he was repulsive. You were so angry you couldn't bear to be near him, and what did he do? Apologise? Ask for forgiveness? He did nothing, he defied you, he believed *he* was King. And then he had Rizzio, your favourite, stabbed to death in front of you. All you did was avenge that.

Mary And now this is him avenging me . . . Jane, you comfort and condemn me at the same time.

Kennedy You had no hold over yourself. You were possessed by love, blinded by mad love for Bothwell. He ruled over you, transfixed you with his magic and sorcery . . .

Mary The power he had was his attraction – that was my weakness.

Kennedy No, he summoned spirits to rob you of your senses. You couldn't hear me warning you, you couldn't see what was happening to you. You used to be so shy and modest but that deserted you.

I remember your face – the desire in it – it was burning red. You were brazen, My Lady, revelling in your shame . . . You let him carry the royal sword before you through the streets of Edinburgh – Bothwell the triumphant murderer . . . The common people followed behind you, cursing your name – I saw them. And armed men – on your order – surrounding Parliament, as you forced the judges to acquit him of Darnley's murder. And then . . .

Mary Finish it. And then gave him my hand in marriage . . .

Kennedy It should be forgotten – left to silence for ever. It was terrible – the actions of a lost soul. But you're not lost – I know. We've grown up together. Your heart's kind, you've repented. Nothing else has blackened your life since. Remember that – and make peace with yourself. Whatever guilt you feel, we know that in England you're not guilty. Elizabeth and her Parliament are not your judges – they're your subjugators. In their court of law you stand courageously innocent.

Mary Who's coming?

Mortimer appears at the door.

Kennedy Paulet's nephew. I'll send him away.

SCENE FIVE

Mortimer enters.

Mortimer (*to Kennedy*) Leave us. Stand guard at the door. I must talk with the Queen.

Mary Jane, stay with me.

Mortimer My Lady, don't be afraid. This is for you.

He hands her a letter. Mary looks at it, taken aback.

Mary What's this?

Mortimer (*to Kennedy*) The door. My uncle must not discover us.

Mary Go! Do as he says.

Kennedy leaves, surprised.

SCENE SIX

Mary, Mortimer.

Mary It's signed by my uncle in France, the Cardinal of Lorraine . . . (*Reads.*) 'Trust Sir Mortimer, who brings you this letter. He is the most loyal friend you have in England.'

Is this a trick? Am I deceived? I thought the world had abandoned me. But *you*, the nephew of my prison guard . . .

Mortimer kneels at her feet.

Mortimer I hate the deception, My Lady, but it was the only way to get close to you. The only way I could rescue you.

Mary Stand. You overwhelm me, Sir – I can't leap from misery to hope so quickly. Explain this to me.

Mortimer Time is short. My uncle will be coming soon with Burleigh to tell you the judges' verdict. But God has planned your rescue.

Mary He's sent me a miracle.

Mortimer May I begin with my part in this?

Mary Speak, Sir.

Mortimer I was twenty, Your Majesty, and raised strictly – fed lifelong with hatred for Catholicism. But one day I had this sudden desire to get away, to go to Europe, to never listen to another boring, puritanical sermon.

I went to France first, then on to glorious Italy, and arrived in the middle of a huge religious festival. The roads were packed with people – it was like all mankind was making a pilgrimage there, to God's Kingdom. I was swept along by this river of worshippers through the streets of Rome. The colonnades, the triumphal arches – the Colosseum! And the art . . .! I'd never felt the true power of art before. My Church hates the senses, it hates stimulation. The image of Christ's body is shunned – they only want to worship the bodiless word.

And inside every church there, the heavenly music . . . And the figures painted on the walls and the ceilings: the birth of Our Lord, the Holy Mother, the radiant transfiguration . . . And I watched as the Pope took Mass, blessing all of his followers across the world. He doesn't need the gold and jewels worshipped by earthly kings, he has divine power. His house is a heavenly kingdom.

Mary Stop. No more. Don't dazzle me with life – I'm imprisoned.

Mortimer So was I, but my prison opened and I was free. I walked from it into the beautiful day of life. And I put garlands of flowers over my head. I swore hatred there and then to the Book of Common Prayer – it's so limited, so dull. I was now one of the believers – and I met others, Scotsmen, Frenchmen. They took me to meet your uncle, the Cardinal – a truly great man, so certain of his faith – and wise and noble. He was born to command the souls of men.

Mary He was my guide when I was young. Tell me about him – does he still think of me? Is he happy? Does he have a good life?

Mortimer He talked with me, told me of the true faith and the doctrines that have to be lived by. He banished all my doubts. Men are led astray by reason, he showed me that. Their eyes must see for their hearts to believe – so the head of the Church, the Holy Father, must be visible to them. What I believed before – they were childish delusions! He destroyed them with his wisdom and eloquence. At his feet, I abjured my past heresies, and then he welcomed me into the one true Church.

Mary His teaching has brought salvation to thousands of people.

Mortimer He sent me to a seminary for English priests in Rheims. I met your exiled supporters there – Morgan and Lesley, the Bishop of Ross. In his house I saw a picture of a woman. It moved me and fascinated me – I couldn't control what I felt. The Bishop told me it was right to feel what I did, that she was the most beautiful woman in the world, but also the most suffering. Suffering in an English prison for the sake of the Catholic faith.

Mary He's still with me, then – I haven't lost everything.

Mortimer You are a martyr. He told me how thirsty England is for your blood – and why. You are descended from the House of Tudor – you alone are entitled to rule England and Britain. Not this unlawful Queen, conceived in an adulterous bed, who, Henry, her own father, dismissed as his bastard daughter.

I've read books on heraldry and talked to legal scholars. All of them confirm this English crown is legally yours – yours by right. This nation that holds you prisoner, My Lady, belongs to you.

Mary This right is the cause of all my suffering . . .

Mortimer When they moved you here from Shrewsbury's castle, I knew it was Heaven's hand, Destiny was calling me – I'd been chosen to free you. The Cardinal blessed me and I set sail and landed here ten days ago.

And then I saw you, My Lady – not a picture – in the flesh . . . This castle holds a beautiful royal treasure. It's not a prison – this is a hall of the gods, more dazzling than the royal court of England. It is an honour to breathe the same air as you. She's right to hide you away. England's youth would rise up and draw their swords, this peaceful island would be outraged if Britain was to see its true Queen.

Mary If only they all saw with your eyes.

Mortimer Saw your suffering too – and your gentleness and your composure. This prison's humiliation can't confine your beauty. You've nothing here, but you're surrounded by light and life. I found it unbearable to have to walk near you, to ignore you, to hide my happiness, my delight at looking at you.

But time's against us – every hour brings the danger nearer. I can't keep it from you any longer.

Mary Has the sentence been passed? Tell me. I want to hear it.

Mortimer The judges found you guilty. Both Houses of Parliament want the execution immediately but Elizabeth's delaying her final decision. Not out of mercy – expediency. She wants to be seen to be bowing to pressure – that her hand was forced.

Mary (*composed*) I expected it – I knew it wouldn't be freedom. So it's to be life imprisonment then . . .

Mortimer No, that's not enough for them. If you live, her fear of you lives too. Your death makes her throne safe.

Mary She'd dare to put me on an executioner's block?

Mortimer She would. There's no doubt.

Mary She's disgracing her royal position – hers and all other kings.

Mortimer She's negotiating peace with France. The Duke of Anjou will get her hand and her throne.

Mary Then Spain will take up arms.

Mortimer She doesn't care about other countries' aggression – as long as her own people are content.

Mary So my head will be given to her people?

Mortimer You wouldn't be the first royal woman – her own mother, Anne Boleyn. And Catherine Howard – Lady Grey too.

Mary The scaffold doesn't trouble me, Mortimer – there are other ways . . . Murder would be easier for them, that's what scares me. Every glass I drink from, I wonder if it's been sent with her blessing.

Mortimer It won't happen, I promise. We're ready – we'll free you. I've twelve other men with me – we received the sacrament together this morning. We meet

18

tonight at Aubespine's palace, the French Ambassador – he knows of our plan.

Mary You don't know what you're doing – haven't you seen the warnings? Babington's head, Tichburn's head – stuck on spikes on London Bridge. Countless other men have died for me too. Go, if there's still time. Burleigh will know of you – he'll have an informer amongst you. You have to leave the country. Defending Mary Stuart brings only misfortune to men.

Mortimer I'm not scared by heads on poles or what happened to all the others. They died, yes, but their names are eternal now. It'd be an honour to die for your freedom.

Mary They're too strong – they've eyes everywhere. It's not just Paulet and his men – all of England stands guard outside my prison. Only Elizabeth's will can open the gates for me.

Mortimer That will never happen.

Mary Then there is one other man.

Mortimer Who?

Mary Lord Leicester.

Mortimer (*shocked*) Leicester? Elizabeth's favourite! The man who persecutes you . . . ?

Mary Go to him. Tell him what you've told me. Take this letter as guarantee – it has my picture inside.

She pulls a letter from her clothing. Mortimer hesitates.

Take it. I've carried it on me for months – I couldn't get it to him because of your uncle. But now my guardian angel has sent you . . .

Mortimer Your Majesty . . . Tell me how . . .

Mary Leicester will do that. Trust him and he will trust you.

Kennedy enters.

Kennedy Paulet's coming – with another man . . .

Mortimer Lord Burleigh. Be ready, my Queen, be calm – you know what he's come to tell you.

He exits through a side door. Kennedy follows him.

SCENE SEVEN

Mary, Lord Burleigh,Paulet.

Paulet You wanted certainty – Lord Burleigh brings it. Accept it with humility.

Mary I prefer dignity – it suits innocence better.

Burleigh I come as an envoy from the Court of Justice.

Mary Lord Burleigh serves the Court with his tongue as well as his spirit.

Paulet You speak as if you already know the sentence.

Mary As it's Lord Burleigh, I do. Get to the point, Sir.

Burleigh You submitted to the Court of the forty-two . . .

Mary (*interrupts*) I submitted to nothing, My Lord. I would never have given away my royal prerogative, the honour of my people and of my son. English law states that the accused must be judged by a jury of their equals – who's my equal in your high commission? Only kings are my peers.

Burleigh You heard the accusations. You allowed yourself to be questioned by the Court.

Mary I listened to the accusations so that I could refute them. Out of respect for them as men – but with none for their office.

Burleigh It's of no matter whether you recognise them or not, My Lady. You breathe English air, you enjoy the protection and benefit of the law and so you are subject to its ruler.

Mary I breathe the air of an English prison. And how have I benefited from your law? I never agreed to abide by it. I'm not a citizen of this kingdom. I am the rightful Queen of a foreign power.

Burleigh And the turmoil caused in your royal name – that should go unpunished? How secure would any nation be if justice's sword could not reach the guilty head of a royal guest as surely as a beggar in the street?

Mary I didn't say I was above the law, I said that I reject your judges.

Burleigh What, do you imagine they're chosen at random from the common rabble? Low-lifes who don't honour justice and truth, who are easily bribed in return for a verdict? The judges are distinguished men of an independent mind, beyond the influence of a monarch, presiding over a noble people, ensuring them freedom and justice. The very mention of their names banishes any doubt: the Archbishop of Canterbury; Shrewsbury, Lord Privy Seal; Howard, Admiral of the Navy. And could forty-two carefully chosen men be corruptible, men who passed your sentence by a majority of forty to two?

Mary (*after a pause*) I'm awestruck. The power of your speech – which is always used so skilfully against me. How can an untutored woman hope to compete with such eloquence? Because if these Lords *were* as you describe them, there'd be nothing else to say. If they found me guilty, my cause would be lost, truly, it would be lost. But these aristocratic, noble men you praise so highly, My Lord, as if you were wanting to crush me with their weight, I see them differently . . . I see them as eunuchs in a harem, flattering each and every whim of their sultan, my great-uncle, Henry the Eighth.

The House of Lords is as easily swayed as the Commons. It passes a law, then renounces it. Ratifies a marriage then annuls it – all at their ruler's command. A daughter's a bastard one day and crowned Queen the next. These worthy men and their exchangeable convictions have seen their nation's faith change four times under four rulers . . .

Burleigh For someone who says she is foreign to England's laws, you are very knowledgeable about its disasters.

Mary My Lord, they say you're loyal, incorruptible, untiring – I believe it. You serve the interests of your Queen and country first, above your own – but it shouldn't be at the expense of justice. I'm sure there are other noble men amongst my judges, but they are Protestants and English patriots, and they're judging me – the Catholic Queen of Scotland!

An Englishman will never show a Scotsman justice – it's an old saying. And an old custom in our countries that no Englishman can testify against a Scot or a Scot against an Englishman. Nature cast our two fiery people adrift on an ocean raft – and then divided it unequally so they'd fight over it. The narrow bed of the Tweed is all that separates us and it has so often run red with our armies' blood. For a thousand years, they've stared threateningly at each other from opposite banks, their swords drawn. Every enemy of England has always had Scotland's support, while the English are never slow to foment civil strife in

Scotland's cities. This ancient hatred will never end until our Parliaments are joined, until one sovereign reigns over the whole island.

Burleigh And that sovereign would be a Stuart.

Mary I won't deny it – yes, I hoped to unite the two nations. Instead I'm the victim of their hate and abiding jealousy.

Burleigh You 'hoped', My Lady, for civil war, for the country to be set on fire. That's how you planned to capture England's throne.

Mary That is not true. I swear by God, I did not. Where's your proof?

Burleigh I did not come here to argue. The Court has found against you – forty votes to two. The Act of Association passed last year forbids any force of arms to be raised in a claim of right to the throne, and that any person who does so will be condemned to death.

Mary That Act, Lord Burleigh, was passed solely for me – it was only ever to be used against me. And the men who worded it are the same men who pronounce my sentence.

Burleigh It was meant as a warning, but you snared yourself in it. You knew the consequences yet you ignored them, corresponding with that traitor Babington and his murdering cohorts, guiding their plot from your cell.

Mary How did I do that? Show me the letters.

Burleigh You were shown them in court.

Mary Copies of them – in handwriting I didn't recognise. You've no proof that I dictated them, absolutely none.

Burleigh Babington admitted it before his death.

Mary Why wasn't I allowed to see him while he was still alive? Why was there such a hurry to kill him before I could speak to him?

Burleigh Both your secretaries, Gilbert Curle and Claude Nau, swore under oath that those letters were dictated from your own mouth.

Mary So I'm to be executed on the testimony of disloyal servants?

Burleigh You yourself called Curle a man of virtue and good character.

Mary He was when I knew him. It may have been the threat of torture that made him testify, not knowing how much it would harm me.

Burleigh He swore a free oath.

Mary Not in front of me!

Two witnesses, my secretaries, are still alive, My Lord – let them repeat their claims to my face. Even a common murderer has the right to that!

Sir Paulet, I know from Shrewsbury, my jailer before you, that English law decrees the plaintiff must be confronted with the defendant. Is it true or did I mishear him? You're an honest man – is it the law?

Paulet It is, My Lady. It is the law. I must speak what is true.

Mary Then why doesn't it apply to me? Why, when it could help me, does it get ignored? Tell me! Why wasn't Babington brought face to face with me? Why not my secretaries who are still alive?

Burleigh You're getting excited, Madam. The Babington plot is not the only –

Mary But it's the only charge that I'm accused of! Don't try to sidestep the matter.

Burleigh It was also proven you negotiated with Mendoza, the Spanish Ambassador.

Mary Stay with what we are discussing!

Burleigh That you plotted to overthrow this country's religion, inciting all of Europe to go to war with England . . .

Mary And what if I did? I didn't – but what if I did? I'm held against my will here, against all laws of nations. Instead of being offered protection I was locked in chains. Tell me, do I owe any allegiance, any duty to this State? Do I owe England anything? I call it self-defence if I make attempts to free myself – using power to meet power. I can appeal to any nation I choose – any course of action is allowed in a rightful war.

But murder – no. My conscience, my pride forbids it. It would dishonour my name. *You* may dishonour me if you wish, but don't judge or condemn me. And don't pretend it's justice, these are the workings of power. A struggle for power between myself and England.

Burleigh You're a prisoner, Madam – you have no power to call upon.

Mary She can exercise her power, she can have me killed, sacrifice me for her security – but be honest enough to call it power! This is not justice – the world will not be deceived. She can have me murdered but she can't *sentence* me to murder! Why hang on to this pretence of virtue and procedure? Tell your Queen to show herself for what she is.

She exits.

SCENE EIGHT

Burleigh, Paulet.

Burleigh So much defiance, Paulet – and she will defy us on the scaffold too. Can nothing break her? No tears at the verdict – nothing showed in her face . . . It's because she knows the Queen's wavering mind – that's what makes her strong.

Paulet Lord Burleigh, her defiance will weaken if we remove the cause of it. Legal procedure was not followed – if I may say so. Babington and Tichburn should have been brought before her. She should have been confronted with her secretaries.

Burleigh No. The risk is too great – her influence on men's minds is too strong. If Curle meets with her, he would withdraw his confession.

Paulet Then rumours against us will start, and the legality of the trial be disputed.

Burleigh The Queen knows this – and it distresses her.

Why could the Stuart not have died before she came to England?

Paulet Amen to that.

Burleigh Or some sickness have killed her in her prison?

Paulet We would have all been better off.

Burleigh But even then, we'd still be branded her murderers.

Paulet People can't be stopped from thinking what they want.

Burleigh Though they wouldn't be able to prove a thing. And it would lessen the clamour they make . . .

Paulet They can make their clamour – what would damage us is if we gave them legitimate grievance.

Burleigh Even God's justice can't escape scrutiny – and public opinion invariably sides with the accused. It's worse because she's a woman. The world will not believe it to be justice. We judges passed our sentence in vain. The Queen has the royal privilege of mercy and she must use it. To let lawful justice run its course would be disastrous.

Paulet So you're saying . . .

Burleigh (*interrupting*) That Mary should live? No. She must not live. No.

This is precisely what keeps our Queen from sleeping at night. I can see it in her eyes. 'To rule in continual fear – or to take the life of my cousin the Queen? Don't I have one servant who'll end my anxiety?'

Paulet It's an unavoidable anxiety.

Burleigh Not, so the Queen thinks, if she had more *attentive* servants.

Paulet Attentive?

Burleigh Who can interpret a silent command.

Paulet What *is* a silent command?

Burleigh Who, if given a poisonous viper to guard, do not treat her as some precious, holy treasure . . .

Paulet That treasure, Sir, holds the good name and reputation of our Queen. It can never be guarded carefully enough . . .

Burleigh When the Stuart was transferred here, the opinion was . . .

Paulet That she was in secure, trustworthy hands. I wouldn't have taken on this infuriating assignment if I hadn't thought it required the best man in England. Don't allow me to think I owe it to anything but my spotless reputation.

Burleigh Word could get out that she's sick, that she's worsening, has quietly faded into death . . . So that she may also die in people's memory. Your reputation would remain unblemished.

Paulet But not my conscience.

Burleigh If you choose not to assist, would you stop another . . . ?

Paulet No murderer shall enter my castle. Her life is sacred to me – as sacred as the Queen of England's. You are the judges. Judge her! Condemn her! And only then will the gates of my castle open – for the carpenter with his hammer and saw to build the scaffold, and for the sheriff and the executioner – no one else. She was placed under my guard – be sure I will guard her with my life.

They exit.

Act Two

SCENE ONE

Westminster Palace. Lord Kent and Sir William Davison meet.

Davison Lord Kent, you've returned. Is the tournament over?

Kent You weren't there?

Davison Duty kept me.

Kent You missed a truly fine spectacle, tastefully devised and nobly presented. We saw the virginal fortress of Beauty and Chastity laid siege to by the forces of Desire. The Earl Marshal, the Lord High Admiral and ten more of the Queen's royal knights were its defenders against France's cavaliers. A herald approached first, singing a madrigal, demanding the fortress's surrender – the Chancellor answered that with his guns, firing from the battlements. Then the French artillery was rolled on, and hundreds of sweet-smelling flowers were fired at the fortress from miniature cannons. All in vain – the assault was resisted and Desire forced to retreat.

Davison Not a good omen for French bridal suitors . . .

Kent The fortress, I imagine, will surrender eventually . . .

Davison You think so? I'm not so sure.

Kent The treaty's been amended – the French have agreed to our marriage terms. Monsieur will take Mass in a private chapel but he will officially honour and observe our State religion. The news has spread quickly – the people are overjoyed. Their fear was always our Queen dying without an heir, and Mary Stuart and papacy claiming her throne.

Davison So the Queen will walk to her bridal chamber, as the Stuart walks towards death.

Kent The Queen approaches.

SCENE TWO

Elizabeth, led in by Leicester. With them, Count Aubespine, Bellievre, Lords Shrewsbury and Burleigh.

Elizabeth (*to Aubespine*) Count Aubespine, my apologies to your countrymen – they must miss the courtly splendour of Saint-Germain. We cannot quite match the Queen of France's lavish celebrations here. But you have seen – to my great pride – my well-mannered, contented people, and how they crowd around my sedan chair blessing me whenever I go amongst them. The glittering beauties who adorn Catherine de Medici's court must draw the eye more than myself and my own humbler merits.

Aubespine To a foreign visitor's eyes, there is only *one* lady at Westminster. And all that's delightful about her sex is united in her.

Bellievre Your gracious Majesty, grant us we may take our leave, to carry back the happy news that Monseiur, our royal master, the Duke of Anjou, longs for. He has travelled on to Paris but men are posted at Calais to swiftly speed your royal consent to his anticipating ear.

Elizabeth Count Bellievre, once again I repeat, press me no further. This is no time to light the torch of marriage. The sky hangs black over our country – mourning dress would be more fitting than bridal robes. A fatal blow threatens to end my rule and my life.

Bellievre Perhaps then, Your Majesty, just a promise that in less troubled days you will fulfil.

Elizabeth Monarchs are slaves to their rank – they are not allowed to follow their hearts. My own desire was always to die unmarried. I would be proud to have people read on my tombstone: Here lies the Virgin Queen. But my subjects are not content – they're already thinking of the time after me. To rule in the present is not enough – I have to sacrifice myself for their future happiness also. For them, I must give up my virgin freedom and have a lord and master forced upon me. This shows me what I am to them – a mere woman. And I believed I had ruled like a man and like a king. I know God is not served well by upsetting the natural order, but I have not been a Queen who wasted her days doing nothing. I have tirelessly, without complaint, undertaken every duty asked of me, and by that fact I should be exempted from the natural law, that law which proclaims one half of mankind should be subservient to the other.

Aubespine Your rule has glorified every virtue, Your Majesty. And of course no man lives who deserves that you sacrifice your freedom to him. Yet if birth, nobility, and courage make one worthy, then that man is . . .

Elizabeth A marriage union with a royal son of France would bring honour to me, Lord Ambassador, I have no doubt of that. If it has to be – if I am to give in to the urging of my people – there is no other monarch in Europe to whom I would give, with less resistance, my greatest treasure and my freedom. Let that be enough admission for you.

Bellievre It is a beautiful hope, but still only hope. My master desires more.

Elizabeth What does he desire?

She pulls a ring off her finger, contemplates it. As she talks she regards Leicester, but with no trace of emotion.

A Queen is no different after all from a common woman. This stands for the same duty, the same servitude. A ring signifies marriage – but it's from rings that chains are made. Take this as a gift to your master. There's no chain yet but from it one will undoubtedly form.

Bellievre kneels to receive the ring, kisses Elizabeth's hand.

Bellievre I receive this ring in his name, Your Majesty.

Elizabeth (*to Leicester*) Allow me, My Lord.

She takes the blue ribbon from his neck to invest Bellievre.

Invest His Highness as I now invest you. *Honi soit qui mal y pense.* May all mistrust between our two nations fade. Let the crowns of Britain and France embrace each other henceforth.

Aubespine Your noble Majesty, this is a joyous day! May it be shared by every person – there should be no suffering on this island. The light of mercy shines from your face. Could perhaps some of it reflect upon an unfortunate princess, a cause of concern to both France and Britain alike . . . ?

Elizabeth Enough, My Lord, you are confusing two incompatible matters. If France is serious about this alliance, it must respect me – it can be no friend to my enemy.

Aubespine But it would be unworthy, surely, for France to ignore a sister Catholic and the widow of our King, François? It is a matter of honour – and of humanity.

Elizabeth Then I acknowledge your country's concern.
while I, England's Queen, will act as such.

*She bows towards the French gentlemen, who retire
respectfully.*

SCENE THREE

*Elizabeth, Leicester, Burleigh, Shrewsbury. The Queen
sits down.*

Burleigh Your Majesty, today you have granted your
people their dearest wish. These are blessed days – we no
longer face a troubled future. Only one sorrow still
bedevils us – one last sacrifice that the whole country
desires. Make it and this day will ensure England's
eternal happiness.

Elizabeth What more do my people wish for? Speak, My
Lord.

Burleigh The head of Mary Stuart. She must be
destroyed so that we no longer fear for your precious life.

Roman Catholicism still has many secret followers on
this island, all of them hostile to your reign, their hearts
loyal to the Stuart. They're allied with the brothers of
Lorraine who make no secret of their hatred for you,
while in Rheims, the Cardinal preaches regicide to his
converts. Three have already made attempts on your life
and many more will try. We all know where they get their
hope and encouragement from – she is sitting in
Fotheringay Castle. No peace can be negotiated with her
and her house – you must suffer these strikes or impose
one yourself. Her life is your death – her death your life.

Elizabeth My Lord, I know you're driven by loyalty,
and I hear the wisdom of your words, but this call for

blood. I hate it with all my soul. Is there no other course? Lord Shrewsbury, what is your opinion?

Shrewsbury You rightly praise Burleigh's loyal vigour – I am equally loyal, though less eloquent.

May you live long, Your Majesty. Your people esteem you for the peace you have brought to this kingdom. Our island has never seen happier times. But that must not be at the expense of our reputation. If that was ever to happen, I hope I will be long dead.

Elizabeth I have no intention of staining England's reputation.

Shrewsbury Then you must consider other ways to save this country – but not by executing Mary Stuart. She is not your subject, you cannot pass sentence on her.

Elizabeth So my State Council, my Parliament and all the courts of this country were wrong to grant me this right?

Shrewsbury A majority of votes is no proof of justice. England is not the world, your Parliament not the representatives of the human race. Today's England is not a future England, as it is any more a past England. Public opinion, the judgement of the people – it constantly shifts and changes. Don't claim it is necessity or that you have to obey, or that it is what your people demand. Your will is free. Make it known you abhor blood, that you want her life spared, that those who advise you differently should bite their tongues. You alone must judge this. Trust your own gentleness to guide you. God did not put severity into women's hearts, and the founders of this nation, who decreed that women could hold the reins of power, they never demanded that severity be a necessary royal virtue.

Elizabeth Lord Shrewsbury, you make a strong case for our enemy – but should I not be listening to counsellors who are concerned for *my* welfare?

Shrewsbury Mary Stuart has no advocate. Nobody dares speak for her for fear it angers you. It is left to me. I am an old man nearing his grave and so it's not from desire for her that I do this. I never want it said that in your State Council compassion was ignored in favour of intolerance and selfishness. Everything conspires against her. You yourself have never seen her in the flesh – your heart is closed to her.

I am not talking about her guilt. It is said she had her husband murdered and that she married the man who murdered him – and, yes, that is a grave crime. But it was committed in a dark, unhappy time, in the upheaval of civil war. She was weak and surrounded by even weaker men putting pressure on her, so she turned to the one who seemed the strongest, influenced by who knows what. Women are fragile creatures.

Elizabeth Not all women are weak or fragile. There are strong souls amongst us – I'll hear nothing of weakness.

Shrewsbury You were raised in adversity, I know. Your early life was not easy or happy. The prospect of death was more real than inheriting the throne. You were confined at Woodstock and in the Tower – that is where your father, our past King, chose to teach you your duty. There were no flatterers or advisers there. You learnt self-discipline, how to apply your mind and think things through, how to evaluate life's true worth.

But God was not so attentive to the other poor girl. She was uprooted to France, still a child, to a court full of pleasure-seekers and drunkards. She never heard a truthful, reasoning voice, instead was blinded by the debauchery all around her. Also she has been given the vain gift of beauty . . . She stands foremost above most women in the world, because of that no less than her birthright . . .

Elizabeth Collect yourself, Lord Shrewsbury, we sit in serious council! Her charms must be extraordinary to set an old man so ablaze. You're very quiet, My Lord Leicester.

Leicester Struck dumb, my Queen, amazed these fairy tales and scare stories have risen from London's streets into the sanctum of your State Council to seriously occupy the thoughts of such wise men.

I admit I'm surprised that this countryless Queen, unable to save her own throne, and a standing joke amongst her subjects, could, in prison, be such a threat to you.

What are you afraid of – her claim to this country? The Guises' refusal to acknowledge you as Queen? How can they take what was yours by birth? Doesn't Henry's last will expressly forbid it? You really think England would embrace a Papist ruler? Turn from their adored monarch to Darnley's murderer?

These are hasty men who press you for a successor, who can't see you married fast enough, to save the State and the Church from mortal danger. You're living in the prime of your youth, while each day she bends closer to her grave, the grave you will walk over for many years to come without your hand having to push her in.

Burleigh Lord Leicester hasn't always spoken this way.

Leicester I voted for her death in court, it's true, but we're in council now, debating advantage, not justice. Her only protector, France, has abandoned her – what's there to fear? Why kill her? She's dead already. Contempt is death – don't bring her to life through pity. I say let the sentence stand. Let her live – but under threat of death. If any arms are raised in her cause, then the axe should fall.

Elizabeth (*rises*) My Lords, I've heard your opinions. With God's help, I will consider them and choose what I deem best.

Paulet enters with Mortimer.

Elizabeth Sir Paulet, whom do you bring before us?

Paulet Your Majesty, it is my nephew Mortimer, newly returned from his travels. He comes to kneel at your feet and offer his loyal vow.

Mortimer (*kneels down*) Long live our royal Majesty. Happiness and glory crown her brow.

Elizabeth Stand. You are welcome in England, Sir. You have journeyed far, I hear.

Mortimer Far enough to win the confidence of all the Scots exiles who plot against this island.

Paulet He has in his possession secret, coded letters meant for the Queen of Scotland.

Elizabeth What do they tell us?

Mortimer They're dumbfounded that France has abandoned them and allied itself with England. Their hopes are now set on Spain.

Elizabeth The same as Walsingham told us.

Mortimer Also, a papal bull has been issued against you by Pope Sixtus. He has excommunicated you and absolved all your Catholic subjects from obedience to you. It arrived as I was leaving Rheims – the next ship will bring it here.

Leicester England no longer fears such things.

Burleigh It will inspire the fanatics.

Elizabeth (*looks at Mortimer enquiringly*) I was told in Rheims you renounced your faith.

Mortimer I did – as a pretence. This is how dedicated I am to serve you.

Paulet brings out Mary's letter.

Elizabeth What is that?

Paulet A letter from the Queen of Scotland.

Burleigh Give it to me.

Paulet Forgive me, Lord High Treasurer, she asked that it be given to the Queen herself. She tells me I am her enemy – I am, but only of her crimes. What my duties agree with, I'm happy to do for her.

Elizabeth takes the letter. While she reads it, Mortimer and Leicester speak in private.

Burleigh (*to Paulet*) What has she written? The Queen should be spared her carping complaints.

Paulet She's requesting a meeting with Her Majesty.

Burleigh Never.

Shrewsbury Why not? It is a reasonable request.

Burleigh She has forfeited any such privilege. She's incited murder, attempted to kill our Queen. Anyone with any loyalty to our monarch could not agree to it.

Shrewsbury And if the Queen wishes it, you would forbid it?

Burleigh The Queen cannot speak with any person condemned to die. The sentence cannot be carried out if the Queen shows her face – the royal presence bestows grace and pardon.

After reading the letter, Elizabeth dries her eyes.

Elizabeth How the fortune of man changes on this earth. This once-proud Queen – how far she has fallen. France's throne is the oldest in Christendom – but one crown was not enough for her – she dreamt of wearing three. But the language she uses now – so different from when she assumed England's coat of arms, from when she let her court flatterers call her Queen of both the nations of Britain. Forgive me, My Lords, it cuts my heart that earthly objects are so insecure, that the dreadful fate of mankind should pass so closely by me.

Shrewsbury Your Majesty, God moves your heart. She has suffered for her guilt – end her suffering. Agree to this meeting.

Burleigh Stand firm, Your Majesty. Don't let misguided humanity affect you. You can neither pardon her nor save her. And you don't want to be accused of vindictiveness – of meeting her so you can gloat over your victim.

Leicester My Lords, let us not overstep our boundaries. The Queen is wise – she does not need us to make the best choice. A meeting of the Queens has nothing to do with the course of justice. It's England's law, not our monarch's will, which has condemned Mary. It's worthy of Elizabeth's great soul that she be allowed to follow the urging of her heart, while justice keeps to its strict course.

Elizabeth Leave me. We will find means to unite what mercy demands and necessity imposes. Now – retire.

The Lords leave. At the door, she calls Mortimer back.

A word, Mortimer.

SCENE FIVE

Elizabeth, Mortimer.

Elizabeth You have shown much courage and self-mastery. Your skill in the art of deception shows a maturity beyond your age, and will undoubtedly shorten your years of court apprenticeship. Fate has called you to a great course, I prophesy it, and, happily for you, I have the power to make my prophecies come true.

Mortimer Honoured Queen, all I am capable of is devotion to your service.

Elizabeth You have got to know England's enemies – the extent of their hate, their tireless bloody plotting. As long as she lives their hope is kept alive. God has protected me until now. Yet the crown on my head trembles for ever.

Mortimer As soon you command it, she will die.

Elizabeth I thought the law would keep my own hand free from blood, but it is by my order she will be executed – and I shall always be hated for it. I must allow it – and I cannot save my name. That is the worst of it.

Mortimer It's a just cause – what does appearance matter?

Elizabeth You don't know the world. Appearance is judged by every man, truth by none. I cannot convince everyone of my right, so I must be careful that my part in her death always stays in doubt.

Mortimer The best thing then would be . . .

Elizabeth Of course, that *would* be the best thing . . . You know what I'm talking of. You are an altogether different man from your uncle . . .

Mortimer (*surprised*) Did you make your wishes clear to him?

Elizabeth I regret I did.

Mortimer He's an elderly man – age makes him cautious. Youth's courage is what is needed.

Elizabeth Then can I . . .?

Mortimer I will lend my hand to your cause. Your name will be saved.

Elizabeth If you were to wake me one morning, Sir, with the news that Mary Stuart had passed away in the night . . .

Mortimer I will not fail you.

Elizabeth When will I be able to sleep in peace once again?

Mortimer At the next new moon.

Elizabeth Farewell, Sir. Do not be sorry my gratitude will have to borrow the cover of night. Silence is the god of happy men – the closest, most intimate ties are bound in secrecy.

She exits.

SCENE SIX

Mortimer is alone.

Mortimer My Queen, you're dishonest and you're deceiving . . . So I will deceive you, I will betray you – it'll be an *honour* for me. Did I look like a murderer? Did I convince you? Did you see it in my face? Trust me as you show off your feigned piety and mercy to all the world while you secretly wait for her to be murdered . . . It only buys me more time for her rescue.

You want to advance me – and I know what reward you have in mind for me . . . As if *you* are reward. Who are you, pathetic woman, and what do you have to give? The vanity of fame and royal favour means nothing to me.

Only Mary has life – she has delight and grace and youth. God is with her. You, Elizabeth, only death is around you. You've never given your heart to anyone – you don't know what it's like – how love invigorates a man.

I need to find Lord Leicester, give him Mary's letter. I hate this. I've no admiration for men of the court. I could save her myself – I could do it alone if I wanted. They'd talk about me for ever, my name, the danger I faced, the prize I won.

As he's about to leave, Paulet enters.

SCENE SEVEN

Mortimer, Paulet.

Paulet What did the Queen want from you?

Mortimer Nothing, Sir. Nothing of importance.

Paulet (*fixes his eyes on him*) You're on slippery ground, Mortimer. A monarch's favour is alluring to the young – don't be seduced by ambition.

Mortimer Wasn't it you, Uncle, who brought me into this court?

Paulet I wish I hadn't. It was not at court that our house attained its honour. Don't sell your soul here, whatever the price she'll have promised to advance you at court –

don't trust her. Once you've done her bidding she'll drop you, she'll deny any knowledge of you, and to protect her own name she'll avenge the murder she herself commanded.

Mortimer The murder?

Paulet Don't pretend. I know what she's suggested. Have you agreed? Have you?

Mortimer Uncle . . .

Paulet If you have, then I curse you. And I relinquish all . . .

Leicester enters.

Leicester Sir, if I may, a word with your nephew. Her Majesty has been kind to him – she desires he be given sole custody of the Lady Stuart. She commends his honesty.

Paulet She *commends*? Does she!

Leicester What do you mean, Sir?

Paulet The Queen is free to trust him. And I'll trust my eyes to keep close watch.

He exits.

SCENE EIGHT

Leicester, Mortimer.

Leicester What troubles Sir Paulet?

Mortimer I don't know. The trust the Queen now shows in me . . .

Leicester Do you deserve that trust, Sir?

Mortimer I would ask the same of you, Lord Leicester.

Leicester You wished to speak in private.

Mortimer If you can assure me I dare do so.

Leicester And what of your assurance to me? Don't be offended – how do I know to trust you? You show two faces at this court – which is the true one?

Mortimer Again, I ask the same to you, Lord Leicester.

Leicester So who'll trust the other first?

Mortimer Whoever's lesser in danger.

Leicester You then.

Mortimer You're an esteemed and respected Lord – I'm nothing compared to what you are.

Leicester True – but to trust you makes me the weakest man at court. A single damning testimony would ruin me.

Mortimer The powerful Earl of Leicester deigns to admit that to me . . . Already I think more highly of myself and can set an example to him.

Leicester Then do it and I will follow after you.

Mortimer (*quickly pulls out Mary's letter*) From the Queen of Scotland.

Leicester (*reaches for it*) Lower your voice! What is this?

He sees the picture, kisses it in silent adoration.
Mortimer watches him carefully as he reads the letter.

Mortimer Now I believe you, My Lord.

Leicester Do you know what she's written here?

Mortimer Nothing.

Leicester But she's told you . . .

Mortimer She's told me nothing. She said you would explain it to me – how Lord Leicester, Elizabeth's favourite *and* one of her forty-two judges, is the same man whom Mary Stuart believes will save her. But it must be true – I can see for myself.

Leicester And why are you so interested in her? How did you manage to win her trust?

Mortimer In Rome I made alliance with the Guises. What won the Queen's trust was a letter written for me by the Archbishop of Rheims.

Leicester I knew of your conversion. Give me your hand. Forgive me my doubts, but I must be careful here. Walsingham and Burleigh hate me. I know they lurk and set out traps for me. You could have been their creature, sent to lure me.

Mortimer It's a disgrace that a great Lord like yourself finds himself so confined.

Leicester You are surprised, Sir, at my sudden change of heart towards Mary. I can tell you I never hated her – but it was necessary I was seen to, due to the circumstances. She was once intended for me – you may know this – intended for me for many years, before she married Darnley. She was radiant then. I turned my back on her – I rejected happiness. Now, I long for her – and I will risk my life for her.

Mortimer A great sacrifice.

Leicester Times have changed. Ambition blinded me to youth and beauty. Mary's hand was too small a prize for me. I'd set my sights on England's Queen.

Mortimer Her affection for you over other men is well known.

Leicester So it must seem – but it's been ten wasted years now, ten years of constant courtship . . . To finally speak it out loud after so many years of frustration.

I'm considered her chosen one, but if they knew how tightly I'm held, how confined I am. I've had to suffer vanity and continual mood-changes; indulge her petty, ridiculous whims. Tenderness one day; pushed aside the next. In favour, then rejected – she has tormented me. Guarded like a prisoner by her Argus eye of jealousy, scolded like a schoolboy, shouted at like a servant. There is no proper word for this Hell I have lived.

Mortimer I pity you, Sir.

Leicester And now finally, after all my wooing, the prize is stolen from me by a young Frenchman. It seems I no longer shine the brightest. Her hand and her favour are taken from me.

Mortimer He's Catherine de Medici's son. They're taught flattery from an early age.

Leicester All my hopes foundered, and from the wreckage of my fortune I reached to grab a lifeline. Mary, my first, beautiful hope. She stood before me again in the full radiance of her glory and youth, and my heart knew what a treasure it had lost, compared to the cold ambition that replaced it. I knew her misery was my fault – it horrified me – and I resolved to rescue her, to possess her again. I got word to her through a friend and told her of my heart's decision. And now this letter is her reply. She forgives me – and if I save her from this prison, she promises to give herself to me.

Mortimer But you've done nothing . . .! You let her be condemned – you *voted* for her death. It took a miracle – in the Vatican in Rome – the light of truth touched me, the nephew of her jailer – it told me *I* was to be her saviour. If it wasn't for me, you'd know none of this.

Leicester Since she was transferred, every path to her has been blocked – and I have a position to maintain. I had to go along with her persecution but I would not have let her go to her death, suffering. I will do everything to prevent that until we find a way to free her.

Mortimer That way's been found, Leicester – as I said, your trust of me would be reciprocated. I will free her – it's why I'm here. My plan's already formed – your support will help us succeed.

Leicester (*alarmed*) What are you talking about? How? What can you do . . .?

Mortimer I will force open her prison gates. I have men ready.

Leicester You have accomplices? What are you pulling me into? Do they know my secret?

Mortimer No. Our plan was agreed on without you, and would have gone ahead without you if she hadn't insisted on your inclusion.

Leicester Assure me my name hasn't been used in this.

Mortimer I assure you – it has not. And why are you so wary about a message which will help you? You want to rescue and possess Mary Stuart, don't you? You've friends now, by your side – Heaven has blessed you. Yet you show more panic than joy . . .

Leicester Force of arms is useless. Your plan is too daring, too dangerous.

Mortimer So is delay.

Leicester Listen to me – the risk is too great!

Mortimer For you who wants to win her! We seek only to rescue her and are less cautious.

Leicester I see nets all around us which will trap us.

Mortimer I have the courage to tear through them all.

Leicester The courage of a fool – it's madness.

Mortimer Better that than your courageous timidity, Sir.

Leicester You'll die like Babington.

Mortimer Do you remember Norfolk's sacrifice?

Leicester Norfolk didn't win her.

Mortimer But he proved he was worthy to do so.

Leicester If we fail, we drag her down with us.

Mortimer If we don't act, she will never be freed.

Leicester You neither think nor listen . . .! You're going to destroy everything.

Mortimer What have you done to save her? I could have murdered her. The Queen asked me to – she believes I will do it today. Tell me how you'd have protected her from me.

Leicester (*surprised*) The Queen gave you that order? And you agreed?

Mortimer So she'd ask no one else.

Leicester Good. This buys us time.

Mortimer (*impatiently*) No, we are losing time!

Leicester If the Queen thinks you're going to kill Mary, she can afford to look merciful. If I could talk her into the meeting, her hands would be tied. Burleigh's right – if the Queen sees a prisoner, the sentence can't be carried out.

Mortimer What will that achieve? The Queen's going to find out I've lied – everything will be the same as before.

Mary will never be freed – the least she'll get is life imprisonment.

This needs audacity – so show it! You've power in your hands – raise an army of noblemen. Mary has many secret allies around the country. There are hundreds of men desperate to be shown a lead. Defy Elizabeth! Show your dominance. Take her to one of your castles – she'll go with you. And keep her confined there until she releases Mary.

Leicester You've no idea what's happened to this country, of how things stand in her court – how tight a hold she has over us. The heroic spirit of our nation's been crushed. A woman has all of us, everything, under her lock and key. You have to listen to what I tell you. Don't rush into anything, do you hear me?

Someone's coming – get away from here . . .!

Mortimer So I'm taking nothing back to Mary . . .

Leicester Take her my vow of eternal love.

Mortimer You can take her that yourself. I'm her rescuer, not your love messenger.

He exits.

SCENE NINE

Elizabeth enters.

Elizabeth Who was with you? I heard another voice.

Leicester It was Sir Mortimer.

Elizabeth You look startled, Sir.

Leicester (*collects himself*) Because of your presence . . . I've never seen you look as beautiful.

49

Elizabeth Why do you sigh?

Leicester I have reason to. To look at you is to feel again the pain of what I've lost.

Elizabeth What have you lost?

Leicester You – and your heart. I have no royal blood but I doubt anyone alive feels more devotion for you. This young Prince of Anjou has never even seen you – he's only in love with a picture and your name. I love you. Even if you'd been born a shepherdess and I was King it wouldn't matter – I would lay my crown at your feet.

Elizabeth Don't, Robert. Can't you feel pity for me? I'm not allowed to follow my heart – it wouldn't be like this if I could. I envy other women who can, who are allowed to love. I'd happily give the crown to the man who moves my heart like no one else. Mary Stuart did – she was free to. She let herself do whatever she wanted. She must have lived a life of joy.

Leicester But now it's a painful life of sorrow.

Elizabeth She didn't care what people thought – she lived carefree. I took on the responsibilities of this office – she never did. I could have lived like her – tasted life's pleasures – but I chose to follow my royal duty.

And so many men admire her, young men, old men, so many desire her – because she was content to be a woman. This is what men are like – their heads get turned so easily by excitement and desire. They lose all respect for what they should revere. Even Shrewsbury – have you seen? – his eyes light up when he talks about her.

Leicester He was her warder. She has bewitched him.

Elizabeth Is it true – her beauty? I hear it so often, I'm curious to know. Paintings flatter and descriptions exaggerate – I could only trust my own eyes. Why do you look at me like that?

Leicester I was comparing you with her in my mind. The pleasure I'd get – if it could be done secretly – to see you standing next to her. The victory you'd have over her – you would humiliate her. She'd see with her own eyes – she'd be forced to see – how much more graceful and noble and . . . You would exceed her in every virtue there is.

Elizabeth But she is younger.

Leicester She doesn't look it. Suffering has aged her. It would be an even greater insult for her to see you as a bride. She has no hope left in her life. If you paraded your happiness as the bride of a French prince to her who's always been so proud of her French family and who's still appealing for their help . . .

Elizabeth I feel I'm being pushed to meet with her.

Leicester She's asked it as a favour of you – make it a punishment. You can send her to the scaffold, but more pain will be inflicted by your superior beauty. That's how to kill her. Your beauty, your modesty, your virtue, your crown – and now to be married. You saw how dazzled I was by your appearance – you are resplendent. What if you were to go to her now, just as you are? There's no better time.

Elizabeth Now? No. No. I can't, Leicester . . . I have to consider it first. I must talk to Burleigh . . .

Leicester (*interrupts*) Burleigh thinks only of what will serve the State, but you as a woman have your own rights. You have to decide, not your statesmen. Though it would be politic to see her, it would be a generous act that would undoubtedly win public approval. Afterwards, you can rid yourself of her in whichever way you please.

Elizabeth It wouldn't be right to see her as she is now – she's not attended. It would hurt me to look at her like that.

Leicester You don't have to be seen by her. Listen to me. You have an opportunity today. The great hunt passes through Fotheringay. She could be granted a walk through the park and you could be there. You would stay hidden.

Elizabeth If this is foolishness, Leicester, it's yours, not mine. But I can't refuse you anything today. I know the hurt I've caused you. This is how favour is shown – agreeing to something that one shouldn't.

Leicester kneels at her feet.

Act Three

The grounds of Fotheringay Castle. Mary runs on. Jane Kennedy follows slowly.

Kennedy You run too fast. Wait for me.

Mary I want to enjoy this freedom. I feel like a child again, running on grass. Have I really been freed from my prison? I want to drink the air – the free, heavenly air . . . !

Kennedy It's still a prison. There's still walls behind those trees.

Mary Then thank you to the friendly trees for hiding them. Let me dream, Jane – don't spoil it. The vastness of Heaven is above us and my eyes can roam at last, far and wide. Those grey mountains covered in mist – that's where my country begins. And the clouds overhead are sailing south towards France like ships of the sky. I wish I could sail with them. Tell France I think of her always! I'm imprisoned, in chains – I have no other messenger. They move so freely across the sky – they can't be held by England's Queen.

Kennedy You're beside yourself. It's this sudden freedom . . .

Mary Look, a fisherman rowing to the bank . . . ! His boat is small but it could save me – it could take me to cities where I have friends. He looks poor – I'd fill his nets with riches. He'd never have to fish again.

Kennedy Stop this – you know their spies watch our every move . . . Even if he wanted to, he's prohibited from coming near us.

Mary Jane, this hasn't happened by chance. This small favour signals a much greater one, believe me. This is Lord Leicester's doing. They'll open my prison inch by inch until finally I see the face of the man who'll free me.

Kennedy I don't know what they're trying to do to us. Yesterday they announce your death, and today this . . . It may be they're giving you your last freedom.

The sound of hunting horns and horses' hooves in the distance.

Mary If I could be on a horse now – be one of those riders. I know that sound so well . . . It's full of sweet, painful memories. I used to hear it in the Highlands, on the mountains, the excitement, the thrill of the chase.

SCENE TWO

Paulet enters.

Paulet So have I finally made you happy, My Lady? Do I for once earn your thanks?

Mary It's you who's done this?

Paulet Why wouldn't it be? At court, I gave the Queen your letter.

Mary You did? Honestly you did? So it has won me this?

Paulet And more . . . There's even more to come.

Mary What do you mean, Sir?

Paulet You heard the horns?

Mary You're scaring me.

Paulet Her Majesty is riding with the hunt.

Mary What?

Paulet She'll be here in a matter of minutes.

Mary trembles, faint. Kennedy goes to her.

Kennedy You've gone pale, My Lady.

Paulet Isn't this what you wanted? What you asked for? Perhaps earlier than you expected. This is not like you, to lose your tongue. Best find it – this is the only chance you'll have.

Mary Why wasn't I told? I am not ready! Jane, help me inside. I need to compose myself.

Paulet Stand where you are. You will wait for her here. I understand it must be difficult to stand before your judge.

SCENE THREE

Lord Shrewsbury enters.

Mary It's not that . . . I feel faint.

Shrewsbury. I can't see her. Help me. I don't want her in my sight.

Shrewsbury Gather yourself, Madam. Have courage. Now is a critical time.

Mary I've waited years for this – prepared myself, rehearsed and memorised every word – to move her, to touch her. Now I've forgotten everything. There's nothing inside me except my hatred, and the burning fire that's my suffering. I have no kind thoughts left. The dark spirits of Hell crowd round me, shaking their serpent hair.

Shrewsbury Nothing will be served by hate meeting hate. Put aside what you feel. She is the powerful one – be humble before her.

Mary I can't do it. I cannot.

Shrewsbury You must! Be calm and respectful. Appeal to her benevolence – do not insist on your rights – now is not the time.

Mary I prayed for destruction and to my curse, my prayer has been heard. We shouldn't meet – we should never meet. No good will come of it. Fire would sooner embrace water or the lamb kiss the tiger . . . I'm wounded too deeply – her offences against me are too great. There can never be reconciliation.

Shrewsbury Stand face to face with her. I saw her moved by your letter – there were tears in her eyes. She is not unfeeling. Take heart.

Mary (*takes his hand*) I wish you were still my jailer, Shrewsbury. I've been treated so harshly.

Shrewsbury Forget that now. You must only show humility.

Mary Is my evil angel Burleigh with her?

Shrewsbury No. Only Lord Leicester.

Mary Lord Leicester?

Shrewsbury There's nothing to fear from him. It was his persuasiveness made the Queen agree to this meeting.

Mary I knew it would be.

Shrewsbury What do you mean by that?

Paulet The Queen approaches!

SCENE FOUR

Elizabeth and Leicester enter with the hunting party

Elizabeth (*to Leicester*) What estate is this?

Leicester Fotheringay Castle.

Elizabeth (*to Shrewsbury*) The hunting party may return to London.

Shrewsbury moves the hunting party on.

The roads are crowded with people. We'll rest here a while.

She glances at Mary as she talks to Paulet.

My people love me to excess. Their adoration is more suited to a god than a human being.

Mary She has a face without a heart.

Elizabeth Who is that lady?

Silence.

Leicester Your Majesty, you are at Fotheringay . . .

Elizabeth (*acts surprised; angrily*) Who has done this? Lord Leicester?

Leicester It has happened, Your Majesty, Heaven has guided your path. Now let its generosity and sympathy do the same.

Shrewsbury Your Majesty, you see before you an unhappy woman, a woman in anguish.

Mary pulls herself together. She tries to approach Elizabeth, but stops halfway, shaking with a fierce internal struggle.

Elizabeth I was told of a woman bent with sorrow and misfortune. I see only pride here.

Mary I will do this – forget who I am, what I've suffered. Fall at the feet of she who's forced me so low.

She turns to Elizabeth.

Heaven has favoured you, my royal sister. Crowned you the victor. I bow to the God that chose it be you.

She kneels at her feet.

Will you not be equally gracious? Do not leave me kneeling in shame. Give me your hand – your royal right hand. Raise me from the ground.

Elizabeth takes a step back.

Elizabeth You are in your place, Lady Mary. I thank the mercy of God He did not deign it to be myself lying at your feet as you now lie at mine.

Mary Human fortunes can change. There are gods who take revenge on pride. Respect them and fear them – it is they who have cast me at your feet.

We both have Tudor blood in our veins – do not disgrace it in front of these men.

Dear God, you're like a rock, harsh and unyielding. Everything – my life, my fate – hangs on my words and tears. My heart wants to open to you – so it can open yours, but your icy expression just closes it up again.

Elizabeth (*cold, stern*) You asked to speak to me. What did you wish to say? I will put aside the insulted Queen and become a dutiful royal sister. Grant you the consolation of my presence. I will be rightfully criticised for showing this generosity to the woman who wanted me murdered.

Mary How do I begin? Find words that touch your heart, not offend it. Dear God, take the sting from what I say and leave its strength. I can't speak for my own cause without accusing you and I don't want to do that.

You have behaved unjustly. I am a Queen like you are – but you've held me prisoner. I came to you, pleading, and you, scorning the laws of hospitality and the rights of nations, had me imprisoned. I have been separated from my friends, my servants. I have suffered humiliating privation. I have been put before a disgraceful court of law.

No. Enough. Let that be forgotten for ever. I will call it fate – neither of us are guilty. It was an evil spirit – it sparked hatred in our hearts – hatred that has been in us since our youth and has grown as we have grown, the flames fanned by evil people and mad zealots. This is the curse of kings – when they are divided, they tear the world to pieces and unleash the furies of discord. But it's only ourselves now – no one can act for us.

She approaches her trustingly, with a gentle voice.

At last, we stand face to face. Speak, sister – speak now. Tell me my crime and I will seek to answer your perceived wrong. If you'd only granted my request to see you before now, this painful meeting need never have taken place.

Elizabeth My good angel has protected my breast from a poisonous viper.

Don't accuse fate – accuse your black heart – accuse the dark ambition of the Stuarts. There was no argument between us until your uncle, the Duke of Guise, that arrogant, power-hungry priest, who stretches out his greedy hands for every crown, started his feud with me. He persuaded you to take on my coat of arms, my royal title, and engage in a fight to the death with me. Who did he not try to turn against me? The tongues of priests, the swords of nations – the terrible weapons of religious hate. Even here, in our peaceful nation, he stirred unrest. But God is with me – your priest has lost the field. The blow he aimed at my head will now strike off yours!

Mary I am in God's hands. You cannot overstep your power like this.

Elizabeth Who is there to prevent me? Your uncle set a fine example of how monarchs should make peace with their enemies – massacre them on St Bartholomew's Day . . .!

Kinship and the law of nations are nothing when the Church of Rome severs the bonds of duty and sanctions the murder of kings. I practise only what your priests teach.

Tell me – what's my guarantee if I were to free you? What lock would secure your loyalty that could not be opened by St Peter's keys? Force is my only security. I will make no alliance with a nest of vipers.

Mary The dark suspicion that afflicts you . . . You've only ever seen me as an enemy; a foreigner. If you'd named me your heir – which is my right – you would now have a loyal friend and a loving cousin.

Elizabeth Your friends are abroad, Lady Stuart, your house is Rome. Name you my heir? While you try to ensnare me with your treachery? Seducing my people, trapping the noble youth in the tangle of your net, dazzled by your new rising sun while I . . .

Mary Then rule in peace . . .! I renounce all claim to this kingdom. You've won – my spirit's crushed, my ambition gone. I'm a pale shadow of Mary Stuart. You've done the worst you could do – destroyed me in the flower of my youth.

End it now, sister Queen – pronounce my sentence. You surely didn't come only to mock me. Say to me: 'You're free, Mary!' Say: 'You've felt my power, now accept my generosity.' One word undoes everything. Give me back my life and my liberty.

You make me wait . . . I'll wait.

If you don't speak, woe betide you. You should leave me with a blessing, like a goddess. For all this island, for all the earth, I'd never stand before you as you now stand before me.

Elizabeth At last, do you admit defeat? Is your scheming over with? No more assassins or madmen striving for a desperate knighthood? It is over, Lady Mary, you will seduce no more of them. No one's keen on being your fourth husband – you kill your suitors as persistently as your husbands.

Mary Sister. Sister . . . God, grant me constraint . . .

Elizabeth So this is the charm, Lord Leicester, which no man can resist and no woman dare compete with? It's an easily earned reputation – to be commonly admired, beauty needs only to be commonly available.

Mary This is too much!

Elizabeth (*laughs*) Now you show your true face. The mask has slipped.

Mary My faults were human – they were faults of youth. I was seduced by power but I've never denied it or tried to hide the fact – I've always refused to speak falsely. The world believes the worst about me but I can say this – I am better than my reputation. But what of you, in times to come, when your royal robes are pulled aside? The virginal robes in which you hide your burning, secret lust. Virtue was something your mother could never bequeath you – virtue *or* legitimacy – we know why Anne Boleyn was sent to her death.

Shrewsbury (*interceding*) In the name of God, must it come to this? Is this moderation, Lady Mary? Is this humility?

Mary Moderation? I've taken all a human being can take. I will not stay calm any longer – I will not be patient. I've suppressed my resentment long enough – it's now broken from its cage . . . He who gave the basilisk its death-eyes, give me a tongue of poison . . .

Elizabeth, in speechless anger, stares at Mary.

Shrewsbury She's beside herself! Forgive her anger.

Leicester moves to lead Elizabeth away

Leicester Don't listen to her! We must leave this place!

Mary The throne of England has been desecrated by a bastard – the British people cheated by a cunning swindler! If there was any justice in this land you'd lie in the dust before me – because I am your Queen!

Elizabeth exits quickly. The Lords follow her in consternation.

SCENE FIVE

Mary, Kennedy.

Kennedy She's furious – you've made her furious . . . It's over. Our hope is gone.

Mary Furious – yes. And with death in her heart. This is a wonderful feeling, Jane. Years of humiliation and suffering – now finally, revenge! I've plunged a knife straight into her heart.

Kennedy That was madness . . . You've wounded her – you went too far. She's the Queen – she'll hurl thunderbolts back at you. You mocked her in front of Leicester, her favourite.

Mary Mocked her? I *humiliated* her! And Leicester was here to see it – how I struck her down. He stood there watching me, giving me strength.

SCENE SIX

Mortimer enters.

Kennedy Sir, it did not . . .

Mortimer I heard everything. Leave us.

Kennedy leaves. He approaches Mary.

What a victory! You stamped her into the dust! You are Britain's Queen – she was like some common criminal. The courage you showed – I was awestruck . . . You're a goddess, a magnificent goddess!

Mary You spoke with Leicester? You gave him my letter, my picture?

Mortimer The magisterial scorn you heaped on her . . . Your presence dazzled me. You're the most beautiful woman on this earth.

Mary Sir, please . . . I am impatient – what did Lord Leicester say? What will happen now?

Mortimer Leicester? Leicester's a pitiful coward. He'll do nothing for you. Forget him.

Mary What are you saying?

Mortimer He imagines he can save you and then have you for himself? He can try but he'll have to kill me first.

Mary You didn't give him the letter?

Mortimer He prizes his life too much. To save you – to win you – a man must be ready to die.

Mary He'll do nothing, then?

Mortimer Don't speak of him. We don't need him. You have me.

Mary What power do you have?

Mortimer I would look to yourself – you're not where you were yesterday. I saw how the Queen left you just now. It's over – she'll show you no mercy. We must act tonight, show courage, risk everything. You'll be freed before dawn.

Mary Tonight? It's not possible.

Mortimer I've men nearby, friends, hiding in a chapel. A priest has heard our confession and granted us absolution. We're ready for our final journey, if this is it.

Mary This is too rushed, this . . .

Mortimer I have keys – I'll let them into the castle tonight. We'll kill the guards and take you from your cell. Everyone will have to be killed – no one can live to tell what they saw.

Mary And Paulet?

Mortimer Will be the first to die.

Mary He's your uncle . . . a second father to you.

Mortimer He dies by my hand. I'll kill him myself.

Mary Oh, this is abominable . . .

Mortimer Our sins are already forgiven. I'm ready to commit the worst that can be committed. The sacrament absolves me – even if I have to kill the Queen.

Mary No, Mortimer, this is too much blood . . .

Mortimer Life's nothing to me without you, without my love for you. I don't care for anything or anyone. The world will end before I abandon you.

Mary The way you talk – the way you look at me . . . It scares me.

Mortimer (*with an unsteady look; a quiet madness*) Life's only a moment – and so is death. They can drag me to Tyburn through the streets, burn me with their irons, tear my limbs apart . . .

He moves impassioned towards her.

I only want to hold you in my arms, my love . . .

Mary Do not come near me. This is madness.

Mortimer Be close to you; kiss the heat of your mouth . . .

Mary In God's name, Sir . . .! I'm going inside.

Mortimer Only a madman gives up bliss, gives up embracing it for all eternity when God has placed it in his hands. I'll save you – even if I end a thousand lives. I swear, as God lives, I'll save you – and then you'll be mine.

Mary Is there no God or angel to protect me? Is this my fate – to be thrown from one terror to the next? Was I born to create nothing but fury? Have love and hate conspired against me?

Mortimer Their hatred of you is as deep as my love. They want to behead you – sever your slender, white neck with an axe. Give the god of love what will soon be taken by death. Your beauty, your beautiful hair – I am your slave for ever. Your willing slave for ever . . .

Mary Sir, the language you use . . . Respect my suffering even if you don't respect me.

Mortimer Your crown has fallen from your head –
you've lost your regal power. Try, issue a command – see
what happens – if anyone rushes to help you . . . You
only have your beauty now – and I'll risk everything for
it. It drives me on, headlong towards the executioner's
axe.

Mary Who'll save me from this torrent of words?

Mortimer Such bravery deserves the greatest reward.
Why should a brave man shed his blood? Life is the
highest good. Anyone who throws it away for nothing is
a madman. You are what I want.

He takes her, pressing her to him.

Mary You came to save me . . .!

Mortimer Show yourself – show your desire. You did to
Rizzio, you did to Bothwell.

Mary Don't speak of them to me!

Mortimer He was a tyrant to you and you fell, trembling,
at his feet . . . If that's how it's done, then I'll . . .

Mary Leave me! You're insane.

Mortimer You'll tremble at my feet too . . .

Kennedy rushes in.

Kennedy They're coming. Armed men – they're
surrounding the castle.

Mortimer (*reaches for his sword*) I'll protect you.

Mary Jane, save me from him . . .

Where do I find refuge? Out here, a lunatic – and inside,
murderers.

Mary and Kennedy rush out.

Mortimer alone. Paulet enters with Attendants.

Paulet Lock the gates! Raise the drawbridge!

Mortimer What's happening?

Paulet Where is the murderess? She must be locked away – the darkest dungeon.

Mortimer What is it?

Paulet The Queen . . .!

Mortimer The Queen? Which Queen?

Paulet The Queen of England – has been murdered on the road to London!

He rushes out.

SCENE EIGHT

O'Kelly enters.

Mortimer Murdered? No, it's a dream – a mad fever of my mind.

O'Kelly runs in.

O'Kelly . . .

O'Kelly Run, Mortimer – escape!

Mortimer Why?

O'Kelly He did it, the madman did it.

Mortimer It's true?

O'Kelly Yes. Now save yourself.

Mortimer She's dead – and Mary has England's throne.

O'Kelly No, she's alive – and it means death for us.

Mortimer Alive?

O'Kelly Her cloak stopped the knife – Shrewsbury fought him off. She'll kill us all. You have to run – they're surrounding the estate.

Mortimer What happened?

O'Kelly It was Sauvage, the Barnabite from Toulon, the one who sat brooding in the chapel while the monk interpreted the papal bull for us. He wanted to take the shortest path, free the Church of God with one stroke – become a martyr. He told only the priest – and attacked her on the road to London.

Mortimer (*after a long pause*) Fate pursues you, My Lady, cruel and relentless. Now you will die – your angel demands your fall.

O'Kelly Where will you go? There's forests to the north, I will hide there.

Mortimer Go – may God guide you. I'm staying here – I'll do everything to save her. And if I fail, my bed will be upon her grave.

They exit at different sides.

Act Four

SCENE ONE

Antechamber. Count Aubespine, Kent, Leicester.

Aubespine How is Her Majesty? My Lords, I am stunned at this act of terror. How did this happen? How is it possible – she was amongst her loyal subjects.

Leicester He was no subject of hers. He was a Frenchman – a subject of *your* King.

Aubespine Then a madman, surely . . .

Kent No, Count Aubespine, a Papist.

SCENE TWO

Burleigh enters with Davison.

Burleigh The death warrant must be written immediately for Her Majesty to sign. Go – there's no time to lose.

Davison It will be done.

Davison exits.

Aubespine (*to Burleigh*) My Lord, I share in the nation's joy. Thanks be to God for preventing this murderous attack.

Burleigh Praise be to Him for destroying their evil intentions.

Aubespine May God condemn the perpetrator of this wicked act.

Burleigh The perpetrator and those who sanctioned it.

Aubespine (*to Kent*) If I could, Lord Kent, I wish to express to Her Highness the best wishes of my master, the King.

Burleigh That will not be necessary, Count Aubespine.

Aubespine (*officiously*) Lord Burleigh, it is my duty.

Burleigh Your duty is to leave this island at once.

Aubespine Leave?

Burleigh You are an ambassador, today your status is protected. That will not be the case tomorrow.

Aubespine And what is my crime?

Burleigh Once I name it, it can no longer be forgiven.

Aubespine As you say, My Lord, I have an ambassador's privilege.

Burleigh Traitors have no privileges.

Leicester and Kent murmur, surprised.

Aubespine My Lord, consider before you . . .

Burleigh A passport signed by you was found on the murderer.

Kent Is this true?

Aubespine I issue many passports. I cannot read each person's inner thoughts.

Burleigh The murderer took confession in your house.

Aubespine My house is open.

Burleigh To every enemy of England.

Aubespine I demand an investigation.

Burleigh I'd fear that, if I was you.

Aubespine This is an insult to me and to my King! He will tear up the treaty.

Burleigh The Queen has saved him the bother. Her alliance with France is over.

Lord Kent, ensure the Count is accompanied safely to the coast. The people have already ransacked his house, where a whole arsenal of weapons was found. They're threatening to tear him limb from limb. It's best he be hidden until their fury's passed. You have responsibility for his life.

Aubespine I turn my back on your country which breaks treaties and tramples on the law of nations. Be sure the King of France will seek vengeance for this.

Burleigh Then let him seek it.

Kent and Aubespine exit.

SCENE THREE

Leicester and Burleigh together.

Leicester So it is broken, the treaty you fought for so strongly. England will give you little thanks, My Lord. Could you not have saved yourself the trouble?

Burleigh My original intentions were good – God has chosen otherwise. Many men have worse things on their conscience.

Leicester We all know when you're sniffing out crimes of state, Lord Burleigh, you get this inscrutable look on your face. You must be pleased – this is a shocking offence and those who committed it still unknown. There will need to be a court of inquiry of course. Words weighed in evidence, glances – even *thoughts* – thoughts themselves put on trial. And at the centre of it all, you, Atlas, carrying all England on your shoulders.

Burleigh You, My Lord, I acknowledge as my master. My eloquence could never achieve what yours is able to.

Leicester What are you saying, My Lord?

Burleigh It was you who persuaded the Queen – behind my back – to travel to Fotheringay.

Leicester Behind your back? When did I ever hide my actions from you?

Burleigh So it wasn't you? You did not want her to go, is that it? The Queen insisted on taking you?

Leicester Say what it is you mean, My Lord.

Burleigh Her Majesty was triumphant in the noble part you forced her to play. She trusted your good faith – only to be viciously mocked and betrayed.

Is this the concern and mercy which possessed you so suddenly in State Council – that the Stuart's so weak and bowed, her blood's not worth spilling . . . It's a good ploy, Leicester – with a sharp point. But too sharp – it's broken in two.

Leicester I will not dignify that with a reply. You'll come with me now and repeat this in front of the Queen.

Burleigh I will see you there, My Lord. Be sure to not lose your eloquence on the way.

Burleigh exits.

Leicester alone.

Leicester I've been found out – he's seen through me. If he has the proof, if the Queen learns there was correspondence between myself and Mary, then I'm finished, guilty, beyond reprieve. Dear God. All my advice to her will be branded deceitful and disloyal – and Fotheringay seen as the final mockery. I exposed her to her hated enemy. She'll never forgive me that. Everything now will seem premeditated, the bitter words she was forced to listen to, Mary's scorn and her triumphant laughter. Even the murder attempt, the last outrageous trick of fate, she'll think I was behind it, that I armed the madman with his dagger. There's no way out, no hope left. Who's coming?

Enter Mortimer.

Mortimer Lord Leicester. Is it you? Are we alone?

Leicester What are you doing? Get away from here!

Mortimer They're after us – you too. Be vigilant.

Leicester Get away! Away from me!

Mortimer They know about the secret meeting at Aubespine's . . .

Leicester What do I care?

Mortimer That the murderer was there . . .

Leicester This is of your own making. How dare you drag my name into it!

Mortimer Listen to me.

Leicester Go to Hell! You claw at me like an an evil spirit. I don't know you. I want nothing to do with assassins.

Mortimer You've been discovered. I came to warn you.

Leicester snorts derisively.

After the murder attempt, Burleigh had Mary's room searched. They found . . .

Leicester What?

Mortimer A letter the Queen was writing to you. Asking you to keep your word, promising you her hand in marriage, wanting to know if you still have her picture . . .

Leicester Death and damnation.

Mortimer Lord Burleigh has the letter.

Leicester Then I'm finished.

Leicester paces desperately as Mortimer speaks.

Mortimer You can still save yourself and her. Swear on oath you're innocent – make up reasons, excuses, anything to stop the worst happening. There's nothing I can do now – our scheme is torn apart. I'm making for Scotland, to recruit new supporters there. It's up to you now – see if your reputation can save you.

Leicester We shall see.

He goes to the door, opens it and calls outside.

Guards!

Mortimer, at first frozen with surprise, collects himself. He stares at Leicester with contempt.

Mortimer Coward. You shameful coward. I deserve it, trusting you. You're climbing over me, using my fall as your bridge. Save yourself! I won't name you – I'll keep my mouth shut. I want no part of you, even in death. Life's the only good the villainous have.

A Guard enters with other armed Guards.

Leicester Arrest this man! He's a traitor. His plot has been uncovered. I will go to the Queen and inform her.

The Guards approach Mortimer.

Mortimer What do you want with me? You're slaves to a tyrant – pitiful slaves . . .! I am free!

He pulls out a dagger.

Guard Take the dagger from him.

They rush at him. He fights them off.

Mortimer I curse you all who have betrayed their God and their true Queen. You broke your faith with Mary, the Queen of Earth and Heaven, and sold yourself to a bastard Queen . . .!

Guard Stop his blasphemy! Seize him!

Mortimer I couldn't save you, Mary Stuart – so I'll sacrifice myself to you. Holy Mother, pray for me! Receive my soul into Heaven!

He stabs himself, falls to the ground, dead.

SCENE FIVE

The Queen's apartments. Elizabeth, holding a letter. Burleigh with her.

Elizabeth He's a traitor. Mocking me in front of his mistress. No woman has ever been so betrayed, Burleigh.

Burleigh What powers did he use, what magic arts, to influence the will of Your Majesty to such a degree . . .?

Elizabeth I'll die of shame. He'll be laughing at how weak I am. I went to humiliate her – and I am the one derided.

Burleigh Now you must see how loyally I advise you.

Elizabeth And I've been properly punished for it. But why *wouldn't* I believe him? He was devoted to me – how could I suspect a trap? Who can I trust when even Leicester lies to me?

I made him who he is – I gave him greatness. He was always the closest to my heart. I let him become my master – King of this court . . .!

Burleigh While he betrayed you for his deceitful Scottish Queen.

Elizabeth The death warrant – is it written?

Burleigh It's ready, as you commanded.

Elizabeth She must die. And he will witness it and then he will die himself. I've purged him from my heart – all love is gone, only revenge now. He has high office but his fall will be sudden and shameful. He'll be a testament to my severity as he was once an example of my weakness. Have him taken to the Tower – I will appoint peers to be his judges. He will be subject to the full force of the law.

Burleigh He will want to speak with you, try to justify . . .

Elizabeth How can he? This letter convicts him – his crime is clear as day.

Burleigh But you are kind and gracious – if you see him, his strong presence may . . .

Elizabeth I will not see him. Never. Never again. Give the order that he's not to be admitted.

Burleigh I will.

Page (*entering*) Lord Leicester!

Elizabeth The arrogance of the man . . .! I do not want to see him! Tell him I will not see him!

Page Your Majesty, His Lordship would not believe me.

Elizabeth I have raised him so high, the servants fear him more than they fear me.

Burleigh (*to the Page*) The Queen forbids him to enter!

The Page exits hesitantly.

Elizabeth But maybe he . . . He could have had reasons. This could be Mary trying to separate me from him. She's cunning – what if she wrote the letter to do just this? Make me mistrust him and ruin the man she hates.

Burleigh Your Majesty, consider . . .

SCENE SIX

Leicester bursts in.

Leicester (*to Burleigh*) So it's you forbidding me to enter . . . ?

Elizabeth This is outrageous . . . !

Leicester I will not be turned away! If Burleigh's received – so will I be.

Burleigh You're very bold, Sir, to storm in here against orders.

Leicester As you are, My Lord, to issue the Queen's orders . . . ! No man at this court gives or refuses me permission on anything!

He approaches the Queen humbly.

I obey only the Queen's word . . .

Elizabeth (*not looking at him*) You're not worthy to be in my sight – get out.

Leicester This is not my gracious Elizabeth – that is *his* voice. My Elizabeth, if she has listened to him, would allow me the same.

Elizabeth Speak then. Worsen your crime! Deny it!

Leicester Can we first have this irritating man leave us? Do you hear that, My Lord? This is between myself and my Queen. Go.

Elizabeth (*to Burleigh*) He will stay. I command it.

Leicester Why do we need him? I want to talk with my Queen, whom I worship. I demand the rights of my position – I insist he leaves us.

Elizabeth Since when do you use such haughty language?

Leicester Since you bestowed your favour upon me, since your heart awarded me this high rank. And what your love gives to me I defend with my life. I'm above him – I'm above them all. He must go. A few moments only – to hear my side of this.

Elizabeth That's long enough to hide the truth.

Leicester That's what *he* has done . . . I want to appeal to your heart, to tell you why I did what I did. Your heart is the only judge I'll accept.

Elizabeth My heart's already condemned you. Show him the letter.

Burleigh gives Leicester the letter. He glances at it quickly, keeps his composure.

Leicester It's Mary Stuart's handwriting.

Elizabeth Read it.

Leicester (*calmly, after he has read it*) So I'm to be judged on appearances?

Elizabeth Do you deny it? Secret contact with her, being sent her portrait,
raising her hopes of rescue?

Leicester If I was guilty, I'd deny it – but my conscience is clear. What she's written is the truth.

Burleigh Condemned from his own mouth . . .

Elizabeth Get this traitor to the Tower. Get him out of here.

Leicester I'm no traitor. I was wrong to keep it secret but my intentions were noble – to expose the enemy, to reveal their plans.

Elizabeth Your excuses are useless.

Burleigh How did you do this, My Lord? Are we to believe –

Leicester It was a dangerous game – but I'm the only one at this court who'd dare play it. The world knows how much I hate Mary Stuart. The rank I hold, the trust in which I'm held must dispel any doubt. I was only showing my duty to you.

Burleigh Why then conceal it?

Leicester You, My Lord, tend to talk before you act, informing anyone who'll listen what you intend to do. That is your preferred way – mine is the opposite. I act first and then talk.

Burleigh Like you're talking now – talking because you must.

Leicester (*scornful*) And you must be proud of yourself – you've stopped treachery, you've saved your Queen . . . You know everything, or so you brag – nothing escapes your beady eye. But if it hadn't been for me, Mary Stuart would now be free.

79

Burleigh Please tell us how . . .

Leicester Her Majesty spoke alone with Mortimer, she confided in him. She wanted Mary killed – something Paulet had refused to do for her. True?

Elizabeth and Burleigh look at each other, taken aback.

Burleigh How do you know about this?

Leicester Your thousand eyes, My Lord, failed to see Mortimer deceiving you. Failed to see he was a rampant Papist – and Mary's lapdog. A fanatic who came here to free her and murder the Queen.

Elizabeth (*in astonishment*) Mortimer . . .!

Leicester It was through him that Mary sent her letters to me – and how I knew of his plan. She was to be freed today, he told me himself as I had him arrested – before he killed himself in despair.

Elizabeth I've been deceived – by Mortimer . . .

Burleigh All this happened just now? After I left you . . .?

Leicester For my own sake, I'd prefer him still alive. His testimony in court would clear me of suspicion. In front of an impartial judge, my innocence would be proven.

Burleigh You say he killed himself? He did – or was it you?

Leicester The suspicion continues . . .

He goes to the door and calls out.

Guard!

The Guard enters.

Report to Her Majesty how Mortimer died.

Guard Lord Leicester summoned me and ordered the knight arrested as a traitor. Mortimer drew his dagger, cursing Your Majesty, and before we could disarm him, he stabbed himself in the chest.

Leicester You can withdraw. The Queen has heard enough.

The Guard exits.

Elizabeth What an abyss of monstrosities . . .!

Leicester So tell me, who was it saved you? Lord Burleigh? Did he know of the danger threatening you? Could he stop it? Your good angel was Leicester – your faithful Leicester.

Burleigh He died quickly, this Mortimer – and so conveniently . . .

Elizabeth I don't know what to say. I don't know what to believe. I think you're guilty but I hope you're not. Will this hateful woman always cause me so much pain?

Leicester She has to die. I vote for her death. I advised before not to execute her unless the enemy rose again. Now, the sentence must be carried out.

Burleigh This is where your advice has got us . . .

Leicester As much as I hate this extreme measure, the Queen's welfare is paramount. The death warrant should be issued immediately.

Burleigh (*to the Queen*) In recognition of his loyalty and sincerity, I would advise Lord Leicester oversee the execution.

Leicester Why me?

Burleigh What better way to rid yourself of any lingering suspicion than to preside over the beheading of the woman you've been accused of loving . . .

Elizabeth (*looks at Leicester*) My Lord advises well. So be it.

Leicester I'd have thought my rank would preclude me – this is a task more suited to a Burleigh than to me. Being so close to Her Majesty I shouldn't deal with such matters. But I will – for my Queen. I will forgo the privilege of my position and take on this hated duty.

Elizabeth Lord Burleigh shall share it with you.

To Burleigh:

Bring me the warrant at once.

Burleigh exits. Noise heard outside.

SCENE SEVEN

Kent enters.

Elizabeth What is this uproar, Lord Kent? What is going on?

Kent Your Majesty, your people are outside the palace demanding to see you.

Elizabeth What do they want?

Kent Panic's spreading through London that your life's in danger, that murderers sent by the Pope are everywhere, and that the Catholics are plotting to free Mary Stuart and crown her Queen. The people are incensed – they'll only be calmed if she's executed today.

Elizabeth So I'm to be forced by them?

Kent They won't leave until you've signed the warrant.

He leaves.

SCENE EIGHT

Burleigh and Davison enter. Davison carries Mary's death warrant.

Elizabeth What do you bring me, Davison?

Davison (*hesitantly*) Your Majesty, you commanded . . .

Elizabeth What is it?

About to take the paper, she recoils.

Oh God . . .

Burleigh You must obey the voice of your people, it is the voice of God.

Elizabeth (*struggling, undecided*) My Lords . . . Is this really the voice of all my people – is this the voice of the world? What if I act on it and those voices then change, those same voices condemn what I've done?

SCENE NINE

Shrewsbury enters.

Shrewsbury Your Majesty, you must not let them rush you . . . Stand strong.

He sees Davison with the warrant.

Has it happened? Has it been done?

That warrant you're holding – it is too soon for the Queen to see it.

Elizabeth Shrewsbury, they're forcing me.

Shrewsbury No one can force you. You are the Queen – order them to be silent. The people are fearful and angry, and you're beside yourself – you are being provoked. You cannot judge this now.

Burleigh Judgement has long since been passed. There's nothing to pronounce – only execution.

Kent enters again.

Kent The crowds are getting bigger. They're getting out of control.

Elizabeth (*to Shrewsbury*) You see how they press me . . .!

Shrewsbury Your Majesty, delay signing. This will determine your future happiness and peace. You've thought about it for many years – don't be rushed by the moment. Collect your thoughts – wait for a calmer time.

Burleigh (*fervently*) Wait, delay, don't rush – while your country goes up in flames, while your enemy prepares to murder you . . .! God has saved you three times from death – today was the closest yet. To expect another miracle would be tempting Him.

Shrewsbury God's wondrous hand today saved your life, and gave me strength to overpower a madman – we owe God our trust and confidence.

You fear Mary alive – but it's her death you should really fear. She will rise from her grave, an avenging spirit who'll haunt your reign and turn your people against you. They hate her now, but not once she's dead. She'll be mourned as a victim of your hate and envy. And when you ride through London, you'll see the change in them, the people who now cheer you. Fear will walk ahead of you through the deserted streets. Because whose head is safe after her anointed one has fallen?

Elizabeth Why did you save my life, Shrewsbury? Why didn't you let the dagger go into me? All this conflict would be over and I could lie in a quiet grave, free from doubt and free from guilt. I'm tired of this reign, tired of this life. If one of us has to die for the other to live, why can't it be me? Let my people choose – I give back my sovereignty to them. I've lived only for their good, not for myself – God is my witness. If they want the happier rule of a younger Queen, this obsequious Stuart, they can have it – I'm willing to step down. I can go back to Woodstock – to its solitude, where I spent my childhood, where there is no royal necessity, where I can be Queen only of myself. I am not made to be a sovereign. They must be hard and unyielding and I am not. I've ruled this island contentedly for many years, serving only my subjects. Now this, my first difficult duty, and look how impotent I am . . .!

Burleigh By God, I cannot stay silent – I would be betraying my country and my duty. You claim to love your people more than yourself – so show it! You can't choose peace for yourself and leave your kingdom at war. Think of the Church – of the old superstitions returning with the Stuart. Think of the souls of every one of your subjects – how you act now means they will either be saved or are lost for ever. Shrewsbury saved your life but I will save England if I have to – that is the greater duty.

Elizabeth I want to be left alone.

No man can offer me counsel or consolation in this matter. I will take it before the highest judge and what He decides I will do. You can withdraw, My Lords.

To Davison:

You will remain outside.

The Lords exit. Shrewsbury stands a moment before Elizabeth. He gives her a meaningful look, before leaving slowly with a pained expression.

Elizabeth alone.

Elizabeth I am my people's slave, ruling in servitude, kneeling before an idol I despise. When will I stand free on this throne? But I must respect the voice of the people and win their favour; satisfy the whims of a mob that only want to see juggler's tricks.

Kings should not have to please anyone or ask for applause for the action they take. I've respected justice and hated tyranny my whole life – and now, when I need to act, my own hands are tied. My own example condemns me . . .! If I was Mary of Spain, ruler before me, I could shed royal blood to my heart's content. But was it my choice to be so just? Wasn't it necessity that demanded it, the scourge of kingly free will?

Only my people's love has held me to this disputed throne. Enemies surround me, wanting to destroy me. The Pope has excommunicated me. I've been betrayed by France's Judas kiss, and the Spanish wage war against me at sea. I'm a defenceless woman fighting alone against the world.

With virtuous behaviour I try to cover the weakness of my claim, the stain on my royal birth by which my father disgraced me . . . It's in vain. My enemies have exposed it and set this Stuart against me, to haunt me like a lingering, malevolent ghost.

No, it must end. This fear has to end. Her head will fall. I want to have peace. She's the fury of my life, a tormenting spirit. Wherever I've planted joy or hope, this hellish viper lies in wait. Coiling herself around my lover, around my bridegroom. Mary Stuart is my affliction. When she's dead, I am free; I am free as mountain air.

The disdain with which she looked at me, as if her eyes could burn me. You're powerless – I am the stronger – my weapon is death.

She walks to the table, picks up a pen.

A bastard, am I . . .? Only while you live and breathe. All doubt about me is destroyed the moment you are. As soon as England can no longer choose, my blood is pure, and I am born legitimate.

She signs the warrant, then lets the pen drop. She steps back from the table. After a pause, she rings the bell.

SCENE ELEVEN

Davison enters.

Elizabeth Where are my other Lords?

Davison They have calmed the crowd, Your Majesty. When Lord Shrewsbury appeared they called him the bravest man in England for saving their Queen. He reprimanded them for their anger and rowdiness. And spoke so powerfully that they went quiet and left the square.

Elizabeth The masses are so fickle, swayed by the slightest breeze. Who can trust them on anything? You may leave, Davison.

As he turns to go, she holds out the signed warrant.

But take this . . . Take it back. I'm placing it in your hands.

Davison Your Majesty, you have signed. You have decided.

Elizabeth I was asked to sign it and I have. A piece of paper decides nothing – a name cannot kill.

Davison But *your* name, Your Majesty, decides everything . . . It will kill like lightning. This orders her execution at dawn tomorrow – it's final. She dies as soon as I hand this over.

Elizabeth Then God, Sir, has placed a weighty business in your trembling hands. Pray that He enlighten you with His wisdom. I will leave you to your duty.

She is about to go. Davison steps forward.

Davison No, Your Majesty . . . I must know your final decision before you leave me. Do you want me to deliver this warrant for execution?

Elizabeth That is a decision that you yourself must . . .

Davison (*interrupting*) I am your servant – I can't make a decision – I can only obey you. The smallest misunderstanding now would mean regicide. Let me be your blind messenger, with no say in this. Make it clear to me what you want. What am I to do with this death warrant?

Elizabeth Its name declares what it is.

Davison So it's to be acted on immediately?

Elizabeth I did not say that.

Davison Then you want me to retain it?

Elizabeth At your own risk – but you will be responsible for the consequences.

Davison Holy God . . . Your Majesty, please, tell me what you want.

Elizabeth I want this business never mentioned again so that finally I may have some peace . . .!

Davison It is only one word. Say it – tell me what I must do . . . .

Elizabeth I have said it – now stop tormenting me.

Davison You've not said anything. May it please Your Majesty to remember . . .

Elizabeth This is unbearable!

Davison Take pity on me. I've only held this office for a few months. I'm not used to the world of courts and kings – I grew up with plain, simple customs. Tell me – make my duty clear to me.

He approaches her pleadingly.

Take it back. Take it from me. It's fire burning my hands. Don't ask me to do this . . .

Elizabeth You will do what your office commands.

She exits.

SCENE TWELVE

Davison alone, helpless, in anguish.

Davison She's gone . . . She's left me standing. What do I do? Do I keep it? Do I hand it over?

Burleigh enters.

My Lord . . .! My Lord, I'm glad you've come. You brought me into state office – now you have to free me from it, from this responsibility . . . Let me go back to the shadows where you found me – I don't belong in this place.

Burleigh What is this? Have courage, Sir. Where's the warrant? Has the Queen signed it?

Davison Tell me what to do . . .? This doubt, this fear of doubt is hellish . . .! I have it – signed.

Burleigh (*quickly*) Give it to me.

Davison I can't do that.

Burleigh What?

Davison She hasn't told me her clear wishes.

Burleigh She's signed it – give me it!

Davison Do I keep it or do I not? In God's name, what do I do?

Burleigh Give it to me. If you delay now you're finished.

Davison And if I act too rashly, I am also finished.

Burleigh You're a fool. You've lost your mind. Give me the warrant!

He snatches the paper from him, leaves quickly. Davison follows after him.

Davison What have you done? Wait! This will mean ruin . . .!

Act Five

A room in Fotheringay Castle, the same as Act One.
Jane Kennedy, dressed in black, eyes red from weeping,
seals letters and parcels. She interrupts herself to pray.
Paulet enters, also in mourning black. Behind him,
Servants carry in gold and silver vessels, mirrors,
paintings and other valuables and set them down.
Paulet hands Kennedy a box of jewellery and an
inventory of Mary's belongings. They all leave again.
Melville enters.

Kennedy Melville. You've come.

Melville We meet again.

Kennedy After such a long, painful time.

Melville A sad, painful reunion. And a final farewell
from her steward to his Queen.

Kennedy Finally they allow her to see her friends – on
the morning of her death. I won't ask how you are or tell
you how we've suffered – there will be time for that later.
Melville, this will be her last day on earth.

Melville Our grief should not weaken us. Today, I will be
strong – promise me that you will too. We'll walk beside
her, heads held high – supporting her.

Kennedy You're wrong to think the Queen needs our
support – she doesn't. She's full of composure. Don't
worry. She'll die as a heroine and as a Queen.

Melville They say she wasn't prepared for how soon it
would be.

Kennedy No. There were other terrors on her mind – not death – her liberator, Mortimer. We were to be freed by him tonight – that was his promise. We spent the night between fear and hope, the Queen worrying if she was right to trust him. Then we heard noises and shouts and banging. We thought it was our rescuers – we were overcome with hope. But then the door opened and it was Sir Paulet. The sounds we'd heard were the carpenters building the scaffold right underneath our feet . . .

Melville How is the Queen now?

Kennedy You can't let go of life gradually. It happens in a moment – but God has granted her the strength – this life to eternal Heaven. She has no fear – and the tears she's wept have been over Leicester's betrayal and Mortimer's death, and the grief of his uncle, Paulet. Always the fate of others, never herself.

Melville Where is she? Can you take me to her?

Kennedy She spent the rest of the night praying and writing her will. She's asleep now.

Melville Who's with her?

Kennedy Her doctor, Burgoyne.

Kennedy makes for the door. Melville moves to accompany her.

Kennedy No, Melville, not until she's ready to see you. I'll tell her you're here.

SCENE TWO

Burgoyne enters.

Burgoyne (*to Kennedy*) Fetch a cup of wine for our Lady.

Kennedy exits.

Burgoyne Melville.

Melville (*embraces him*) Burgoyne. Is the Queen strong?

Burgoyne She says she is, but her courage deceives her. She needs some sustenance for what lies ahead. We can't have them boasting that the fear of death made her face so pale, when it is only weakness and fatigue.

SCENE THREE

Kennedy enters, carrying a cup of wine.

Melville What is it?

Kennedy Oh God . . . I was on the staircase to the lower hall . . . A door was open – I looked inside . . . Oh God.

Melville Calm yourself.

Kennedy Everything's covered in black cloth – the walls, the scaffold . . . There's a black block with a cushion and an axe – the blade caught the light as I passed. And people are crowding around it, waiting, wanting blood, wanting our Queen.

SCENE FOUR

Mary enters, dressed in white. She wears a coronet in her hair and carries a crucifix. Around her neck is an Agnus Dei on a row of small beads; a rosary hangs from her belt. Melville sinks involuntarily to his knees. Mary looks at them all calmly.

Mary Don't be sad. Don't cry. You should be rejoicing with me – my suffering will soon be over. My chains will fall from me, my prison open and my soul will be carried to Heaven on angels' wings. Death comes to me now as a friend, comforting, healing, covering my dishonour in its black wings. No matter how low he's fallen, man's made noble again by death. I feel the crown on my head once more – and pride and dignity in my soul.

Melville . . . Stand, Sir, stand. You're going to witness my triumph, not my death. This is a blessing – that my reputation will not be solely in the hands of my enemies. You have come, a believer of my faith, who'll stand beside me in the hour of my death.

Tell me how you've survived in this hostile country? My heart has feared for you.

Melville My only pain has been my grief for you and my inability to serve you.

Mary How is Didier, my chamberlain? Though he was old when I last saw him – has he passed on?

Melville God has not granted him that favour yet – he still lives, to see you buried in your youth.

Mary I wish before death I could have kissed the faces of my family – instead I am to die amongst strangers.

My final wishes, Melville, for those I love. I bless my royal brother, the most Christian King and his royal house of France. I bless my uncle, the Cardinal, and my cousin, Henry Guise. I also bless the Pope, the Holy Governor of Christ, who has blessed me, and the Catholic King of Spain who offered to be my saviour and my avenger. Each is named in my will – and given modest gifts of my love.

She turns to her servants.

I've written to the King of France – he'll offer you sanctuary there. I urge you to leave this country as soon as I'm gone – the English will only revel and gloat in your misery. On this crucifix, promise me you will.

Melville (*touching the crucifix*) I swear to you in the name of us all.

Mary I trust they'll honour my will and share these belongings amongst you. Jane, my loyal Jane – I bequeath this to you.

She hands Kennedy a scarf.

I embroidered it myself – so many tears are woven into it. When it's time, cover my eyes with it. This is the last service I will ever ask from you, my beloved Jane.

Kennedy Melville, I can't bear this . . .!

Mary Come.

She stretches out her hands. Jane goes to her.

Go now.

She turns away from them. Kennedy and Burgoyne leave. Melville stays.

SCENE FIVE

Mary, Melville.

Mary Everything's arranged – I leave this world in debt to no one. Only one thing, Melville, still weighs on my soul.

Melville Tell me.

Mary I am on the edge of all eternity. I will soon stand before God, the Highest Judge, but I haven't yet made my peace with Him. They wouldn't allow me a priest of my own Church – and I refused to take the sacrament from their false men of God. I have to die in the faith and sure salvation of our universal Catholic Church.

Melville Be calm. Heaven will have seen your desire – and how they have denied it. It's the heart's devotion that God seeks. The spirit's faith tells Him more than any word.

Mary The heart's not enough, Melville. Faith needs to show itself on earth. It's why God became a man – he wanted to seal his unseen, heavenly power into a visible body that other men might see. When thousands worship together embers become flames and that is when the soul, inspired, soars upwards to Heaven. They are lucky who can gather together and pray in the House of the Lord. It's this I've been denied. Heaven's blessing will never reach my prison cell.

Melville It will reach you – it's close to you. Trust the Almighty – He made the barren staff grow leaves, He brought water from a rock. He can make an altar in this prison and turn this earthly wine into heavenly blood.

He takes the cup of wine from the table.

For you, God can deliver a miracle. No priest, no Church, no Body of the Lord? There is – before you now.

Melville takes from his coat a Host on a golden dish.

I am your priest – I will hear your last confession, and allow you to make your peace with God. I bring you this Host, blessed by the Holy Father himself.

Mary Heaven's messenger has come to me when every earthly rescuer has failed me. I kneel before you as you used to kneel before me.

Melville makes the sign of the Cross over her.

Melville In the name of God the Father, the Son and the Holy Ghost. Mary Stuart, have you examined your heart, do you vow and swear to confess the truth before the God of truth?

Mary My heart is open before you and Him.

Melville What sin weighs on your conscience since you last were reconciled with God?

Mary My heart has been full of hate and thoughts of revenge. I tried but I couldn't forgive my enemy.

Melville Do you repent this sin? Do you truly wish to leave this world in peace?

Mary As truly as I pray that God forgives me.

Melville What other sin does your heart accuse you of?

Mary Sinful love. My heart was drawn to a man who left me and deceived me.

Melville Do you repent? Has your heart turned now to God?

Mary I struggled – but I won.

Melville What other sin does your conscience accuse you of?

Mary A guilt I've confessed before – it still haunts me. I agreed to my husband's murder – Darnley, the King. I'd given my heart to the seducer, Bothwell – and afterwards, I married him. I've tried to atone for it but my soul has never let me.

Melville Does your heart accuse you of any other sin not yet confessed?

Mary You've heard everything that burdens my heart.

Melville Remember the Almighty is near. The Holy Church punishes an incomplete confession – it is a sin against the Holy Spirit.

Mary I haven't knowingly kept anything from you.

Melville What about the crimes you're being punished for here? Your part in Babington's plot. You are to die on earth for it – do you also want to die eternally?

Mary In less than an hour, I will face eternity – I will stand before His throne. I say it again: my confession is complete.

Melville Consider it well. The heart deceives us. You may, with unknowing equivocation, have avoided the word which makes you guilty, although your will was party to the crime. You cannot trick the eye of fire that gazes searchingly into our hearts.

Mary I called on all monarchs to free me but I never, by intent or deed, made an attempt on my enemy's life.

Melville Then your secretaries lied?

Mary It's as I said. Their testimony is for God to judge.

Melville You'll climb the scaffold, then, sure of your innocence?

Mary By my undeserved death, God is making me atone for my earlier crime.

Melville (*makes the sign of the Cross over her*) Go then and make atonement by your death. Be a willing sacrifice upon the altar. Blood offered will redeem what blood committed. It was your frailty that made you sin, but that frailty will not accompany you to Heaven. I now here, by virtue of the power given to me, do grant the absolution of all your sins.

He hands her the Host.

The body of Christ which was given for you.

He takes the cup, consecrates it with silent prayer, then hands it to her. She hesitates to take it.

98

The blood of Christ that was shed for you. Take it. It is the privilege only of kings and priests, but the Holy Father has granted you this favoured grace.

She takes the cup.

As your earthly body is joined with God, so will you be there in His Kingdom of joy where no guilt or tears reside.

He puts down the cup. At a noise heard outside, he goes to the door, returns.

Melville You have one last ordeal. Can you conquer your feelings of bitterness and hate?

Mary Yes. I've sacrificed my hate and my love to God.

Melville Lord Leicester and Lord Burleigh are here.

SCENE SIX

Burleigh, Leicester and Paulet enter. Leicester stays in the background, not raising his eyes. Burleigh, who watches his behaviour, steps between him and Mary.

Burleigh Lady Stuart, I come to hear your final commands.

Mary Thank you, My Lord.

Burleigh It's Her Majesty's wish that nothing reasonable is denied you.

Mary I've given my will to Sir Paulet. My last wishes are there – I pray that they're honoured.

Paulet You have my word.

Mary I want no harm to come to my servants – they're to be sent to Scotland, France or any other country of their choice.

Burleigh As you wish.

Mary And since I will not be buried in consecrated ground, I ask that Melville be allowed to carry my heart back to France, to my family – where it has always been.

Burleigh It shall be done. Do you have other . . . ?

Mary Tell my sister Queen that I forgive her my death with all my heart, and I ask her forgiveness for my anger yesterday. May God bless her and grant her a prosperous reign.

Burleigh Do you still refuse to see a dean of our Church?

Mary I've made peace with my God.

Sir Paulet, I did not want to, but I've caused you much pain. I hope you will not remember me with hatred.

Paulet (*gives her his hand*) God be with you! Go in peace!

SCENE SEVEN

Jane Kennedy enters. She's followed by the Sheriff, holding a white staff. Beyond him, through the open door, armed men.

Mary What is it, Jane? The time has come. Melville, Jane, walk with me.

To Burleigh, who indicates they can't:

Surely you'll allow me this . . . ?

Burleigh I have no authority to.

Mary I'm a woman about to climb the scaffold – I don't want to be roughly handled by men I don't know. This can't be my royal sister's wish.

Burleigh No women are allowed – their weeping and wailing is . . .

Mary Jane will not weep, I give you my promise. Do not separate me from my loyal friend. I want her hand to lead me to my death.

Paulet (*to Burleigh*) Let her.

Burleigh Very well.

Mary Then nothing else holds me in this world.

She takes the crucifix, kisses it.

My Saviour and Redeemer! As you opened your arms on the Cross, open them now to receive me.

She moves forward, meeting the eye of Leicester. Mary weakens, about to fall. Leicester catches her.

You kept your word, Lord Leicester – you promised you'd lead me from this prison on your arm . . .

He can hardly look at her. She speaks quietly.

And how precious freedom would have been, on your arm, in the warmth of your love, at the beginning of a new life. I'm leaving this world, leaving behind earthly temptation. I can say without blushing now, Leicester, I've overcome my weakness for you. Farewell – and if you can, live a happy life. You sought the love of two Queens, and betrayed – sacrificed – my gentle loving heart for her proud one. Go to Elizabeth, kneel at her feet – may your reward not prove your punishment. Now I've nothing more on this earth.

Mary exits with Jane and Melville by her side. Burleigh and Paulet follow after them.

SCENE EIGHT

Leicester stays behind, alone.

Leicester And I am still alive. But how can I bear to live?

If this roof could fall now, crush me with its weight. Or the ground to open at my feet and pull me down. What have I lost? What treasure have I thrown away? She's gone, a soul already transfigured – and for me, only the despair of the damned.

I told myself I'd feel nothing, I'd smother the voice of my heart. Watch indifferent as her head fell. Was it the sight of her? Did it wake my shame? Is she in death pulling me closer to her? Fool, don't be touched by womanly pity. You were never to have the happiness of love. Cover your body in armour, make your heart a rock. You don't want to lose the prize – stand strong – be brave. Forget pity. Turn your eyes into stone. I must watch her – I must witness it.

He walks towards the door, stops.

No. I can't. I can't look at her. I can't watch her die.

He hears noises below, stares at the floor.

They're down there, under me, underneath my feet. It's started . . . Voices. I have to leave here. I have to leave this place of death.

He tries to exit through another door, but it's locked.

Has God imprisoned me? Does he want me to listen to this . . . ?

That's the dean's voice . . . She's interrupted him. She's praying – her voice is so strong . . .

It's quiet. Her maid's removing her robe. The stool moved closer to the block. She's kneeling down on the cushion. She's laying her head down . . .

He stops speaking, shudders. From below the muffled voices continue.

SCENE NINE

The Queen's apartments. Elizabeth enters from a side door, restless.

Elizabeth No one comes – no one brings me news . . .

Is day never going to come? Will the sun never rise? How long do I have wait on this torture rack of expectation? Is it done or is it not done? I don't want to ask – the thought of either makes my body shudder . . .

Lord Leicester hasn't shown himself – or Burleigh . . . If they've left London, then it's been done, the arrow has left the bow and has flown and has struck its mark. It was for my realm – I could not have stopped it. Who is there?

SCENE TEN

Kent enters.

Elizabeth Where are my other Lords?

Kent Lord Burleigh and Lord Leicester . . .

Elizabeth (*tense*) Where are they!

Kent No longer in London.

Elizabeth Then where?

Kent I don't know, Your Majesty. Both left the city before dawn.

Elizabeth I am the Queen of England!

She paces, agitated.

Leave me! Summon . . . No, stay . . . !

She's dead. At last I have room on this earth. Why am I trembling? The grave's ended my fear – and who'll dare to say I did it? I'll show no lack of tears for her.

You're still here? Summon Davison immediately. And bring me Lord Shrewsbury – no, he approaches . . .

Kent exits.

SCENE ELEVEN

Elizabeth, Lord Shrewsbury.

Elizabeth Welcome, My Lord. What brings you here at this hour?

Shrewsbury My concern for your good name, your Majesty. I have just come from Mary's secretaries in the Tower. I wanted to hear their testimony again to test its truth. The governor refused to let me see them – I had to threaten him. And then what I saw there . . . Curle lay on his bed as if beset by furies, his hair unruly, his eyes madly staring. When he saw me he began screaming and clawing at me, begging to hear about Mary. A rumour had got round she was condemned. I told him it was true – and by his testimony. He started beating himself, pounding his chest with his fists, cursing himself to hell for giving false evidence. He swore the Babington letters were forged. He ran to the window and shouted it into the streets below . . . He'd wrongly accused her.

Elizabeth He's out of his mind – you said so. The raving of a madman proves nothing.

Shrewsbury The force of his madness cannot be ignored. I beseech you, Your Majesty, demand there be a new inquiry.

Elizabeth Very well, I will – because you want it, not because I believe my peers have judged them wrongly. I'm glad there's still time. I want no shadow of doubt falling across my royal honour.

SCENE TWELVE

Davison enters.

Elizabeth Sir, the warrant I gave to you, where is it?

Davison (*astonished*) The warrant . . . ?

Elizabeth Which I gave you for safe keeping.

Davison stares at her, afraid.

The people wanted me to sign it and I did – I was forced to. But I asked you to safeguard it to gain time. You remember? That is what I told you. So now, give it to me.

Shrewsbury Hand it over, Sir, matters have moved on. There is to be an inquiry.

Elizabeth What's wrong with you? Where is the warrant?

Davison (*despairingly*) I'm finished. I'm dead.

Elizabeth I hope, Sir, you have not . . .

Davison I no longer have it.

Elizabeth What has happened to it?

Davison Lord Burleigh has it. Since yesterday.

Elizabeth This is how you obey me? Did I not order you to keep it in your care?

Davison No, that was not what you told me, Your Majesty.

Elizabeth So I'm lying, you wretch? When did I order you to give it to Burleigh?

Davison Not in certain, clear words – but . . .

Elizabeth You have the gall to interpret my words? To put your own low meaning into them? That is your great misfortune – you shall pay for this with your life. You see how my name is abused, Lord Shrewsbury.

Shrewsbury I do. My God . . .!

Shrewsbury If Burleigh acted on his own authority, without your knowledge, he will have to explain himself before the Court of Peers. History will accuse you for what he has done.

SCENE THIRTEEN

Burleigh enters, bows before the Queen.

Burleigh Long live my royal mistress, And may all enemies of England die like the Stuart.

> *Shrewsbury turns his face away. Davison looks on in despair.*

Elizabeth Tell me, Sir, did you receive the warrant from my hand?

Burleigh No, Madam. From Davison.

Elizabeth Did Davison hand it to you in my name?

Burleigh No. He did not.

Elizabeth And you carried it out without knowing my will?

The sentence was just, the world cannot blame us, but you were wrong to act faster than our heart's mercy. Remove yourself from our presence.

To Davison:

Your commission was a sacred pledge entrusted to you. You shall be taken to the Tower. I want capital charges brought against him.

Shrewsbury, you are the most just adviser I have. From now on, you shall be my guide, my friend.

Shrewsbury Do not expel men who have been loyal to you or men who have acted on your behalf and kept silent about it.

For myself, Your Majesty, I must return to you the Seal of England I've been entrusted with for twelve years.

Elizabeth (*stunned*) No, Shrewsbury! You cannot leave me now . . .

Shrewsbury Forgive me, I'm too old in years, and my straight hand, it is too stiff to seal your recent deeds.

Elizabeth The man who saved my life is leaving me?

Shrewsbury I did not do much – and not enough to save your noble side. Live and reign well. Your rival Queen is dead. There's nothing more to fear now – nothing more you need respect.

He exits. Kent enters.

Elizabeth Send for Lord Leicester!

Kent Lord Leicester asks to be excused. He is on board a ship to France.

Elizabeth restrains herself from showing emotion and stands calmly composed.

End.